OUT
SPOKEN
PRESS

Published by Out-Spoken Press,
Future Studio,
237 Hackney Road,
London, E2 8NA

The rights of Fran Lock to be identified as the author of
this work have been asserted by them in accordance with
section 77 of the Copyright, Designs and Patents Act 1988.

A CIP record for this title is available from
the British Library.

First edition published 2019
ISBN: 978-1-9160468-5-6

Artwork:
Ben Lee

Printed & Bound by:
Print Resource

Typeset in: Baskerville

Out-Spoken Press is supported using
public funding by the National Lottery
through Arts Council England.

Fran Lock
Contains Mild Peril

Acknowledgements

Thanks is due to *Bad Betty Press, Black Light Engine Room Press, Blue of Noon, The Chicago Review, Culture Matters, The Curly Mind, Disclaimer Magazine, The Lampeter Review, Mechanics Institute Review, The Morning Star, One Hand Clapping, POETRY, Poetry Bus, Poetry London, Poetry Wales, Poetry Review, Proletarian Poetry*, and *The Rialto* where some of these poems first appeared.

Contents

*

Introduction

The title of this collection is taken from a 'consumer advice line', one of those descriptions supplied by the BBFC and slapped on the back of your DVDs in order to clarify the classification of a particular film. Some of these are gloriously silly. *Harry Potter and the Chamber of Secrets*, for example, features 'mild language and fantasy spiders'. Another favourite of mine is 'moderate torture'. In what sense can *torture* be said to be moderate? I did consider this last as an alternative title, but there's having a sense of humour about yourself, and then there's issuing a gilt-edged invitation to ridicule.

The title poem was originally named something else altogether, I forget what. But after sharing the poem one Wednesday night at Poetry School, and explaining the line 'my face is a fifteen certificate' in terms of the BBFC's 'mild peril' descriptor, I was advised by Roddy Lumsden to change it. Roddy was right. Naturally. Other 'mild peril' poems came out of that class of his, of which Alex Bell's was / is the best. I often found this to be the case.

But I take credit — if such is due — for the notion of 'mild peril'. I like it and I think it stuck with people because it seems to say something about our collective precarity; the apprehen-sion, threat, and unspecified dread with which all of us live. Some more than others, obviously.

Last exit to Luton

He's a real man, you can tell, all plushy skunk and a dog you'd do well
to avoid. Aaron's twenty-three; says he could wear my moony face
as a pendant, calls me *tweety-bird*. I hang around his neck and Aaron drives.
He's taking me out to get buzzed at a club. I'm wearing white denim, spotless
as a chorister, and we are sculling the druggy gale between the tyre shop
and the roundabout; we're leaving these scutty streets, with their pawned gold
and thawed meat, far behind us. We're away up the town, gone for the gavelled
abandon of *smashed out me 'ead*, for fighting *squib* with *binge*, and living
for the weekend.

Aaron is not like the boys at home, dimbulb chinless wonders who only
want to trap you in the maundering bondage of marriage like their mothers.
Aaron's got other ideas, got big ideas, and vodka, and jellies, and he understands.
I'm *mature*; need more than pliant writhing in a narrow bed that howls
like a chimney. He says *you're better than them*, and he's right. I refuse to end up
like that, like the girls at the camp, lank slags currying love and desperate quaking
from spousal apathy; to be one of life's pale remainders, scrubbing my sink and trudging
to church, burnt out on a soused downer again. I don't want to be tied to the site,
to the tribe, to the old men, their tournaments and sorceries; to a fist in the face. I am
special. I am rare. I want gilt and spree and perfect hair and endless fucking diamonds.

He will take me away, I know it. In the club we are spinning until my vision
breaks into dizzy splinters; his kisses determine directionality. I'm lipping
limoncello, lisping citronella, reeling round my handbag like a wasp around
a bin. I see myself in the mirrored ceiling, well impressed with the brittle shimmy
of me. Aaron is grinning, and I am watching the weaponised swag of my nails, rinsed
in warm red light and raving in front of my face, my own face, big as a billboard. All is
love, and there is God, shining like a migraine!

He will take me away, he says, but not today. Tonight it is back to his flat
by flickering inches, and then to bed, this mad cabbagey firmament, where I
am rummaged and squirreled by turns. Aaron is smoking, the smoke hangs
in the air like a spookhouse special effect. His back is baroque with spots,
a constellated mire. He does not tell me that he loves me, he tells me I am *old
for my age*, and I smile. I smile at his Jesus tattoo, pink and coy as a bearded
lady. Jesus is smiling too. I have no plans. I don't want to go home. I have
school in the morning. You know what they say about gypsy girls: our life
is either a circus or a zoo.

A rough guide to modern witchcraft

For Roddy

To begin with, an incision in the blanched cerebellum of a cauliflower,
a pale obol of hot fat. Open up the pomegranate's ripe encrusted lung;
wrap your amulets of garlic in the white chantilly crepe of tripe. Take
any human heart, and pierce with dark projectiles of asparagus. Forge
bright ingots of chilli on anvils of meat. Bake strands of your own coarse
hair into this bullion-darkest rye to give it better strength.

To begin with, hunger is a wrinkle in the breath. Fortune is the black
plough that turns up tea. Everything has meaning: the bones you soak
for soup, the slippery white ganglion of a soft-boiled egg; thin fuses
of vanilla. Condense a broth of cloves and shoots; of arrowheads
and thunderstones. A hole in a steak like a jewellers' loupe. Through
it you can see your future drip and spread.

To begin with, seasoning and yeast. To begin with, spinning in
your kitchen, barefoot after midnight, measuring your cannibal
proclivities against the reddest bite of bitter fruit. This is the spell:
your hands in iridescent gloves of borrowed scales; a yellow lace
of pasta, sighing in an eyelet. This is the spell: the grapes we tread
to lustre. The charm by which we're well.

Precarity

For Jack

The parcels I send simply do not arrive. It is winter.
The house has been pregnable, cold. I leave the city in order
to speak of a rare, inevitable light; to tell you of contorted
skies above grim silos. Silence. Love is sufficient but brittle,
it always was. Most utter mercy, Grace of God, aimlessness.
These things I wish for you. Luck isn't wine, it won't improve
with age, but still. You and I keep the same feasts, my friend:
obscure saints with improbable powers. Our desires are likely
too simple. The rabbit's foot dangles, intent upon chance.
We should have asked for the moon. Hold up your hand.
The needy span of claret in a flashlight, an aggravated purity,
something sore and hurt. How do I love you? Like Christ, his
upturned dumpling face afloat in the golden miso of his own
holiness. Young and born, sunblessed and remedial-exquisite.
My love is harrowed treasuring, devoted and fanatical. That is
to say that we'll have no half measures here. That is to say,
and how much water can a lung hold? That I would drink
the mid-Atlantic all unsteady, ride the rooftops bareback into
sleeplessness. That is to say, I am here, present but meagre,
with nothing else to send but love. Condition the day to walk
at heel, and think about you, often, as brave as the climate,
facing things. What fills me now is admiration. Hardy, still,
you are, and singing.

The Rites of Spring

Long day awash with wheezing breath, sadsoft
mood of lesser nettles, heading home at five a.m.
Our mutant cohort treading weather, unkempt
earliness we walk, in transports, tribal blankets,
pixie-hooded, resolute. Come again to London:
affrighted sky, beleaguered wage, the rage we
bargain into grief. Count the ribs of half-starved
dogs while city women shriek like zips. This is
spring, the whole world running with green
scissors, a cockadoodle spite beneath their skin.
Back again, pacing the sprained light of squats,
reeling a love we want to dig the loamy breadth
of. Back, to days spent lying better-dead against
the corkscrew guts of mattresses. This is spring,
Neanderthal with suffering, and twitching
its teased prick. And we will seek dark spaces,
fold our arms like pharaohs, close our eyes until
fury's gold implosion finds us, sunshine after
cinema. *Then* we will rise, practise our pagan
ablutions: boys in stonewashed mood swings,
grinning a dissolute wonder, girls atilt with
a sauntering kilter, singing to cheap speed,
adrenal distress; old men leading their
horses to water, and all the lust they're lame
and fumbled with. We will honour you, ghost,
with vodka bottles smashed for making rainbow
mincemeat out of daylight. We will honour you,
with three part harmonies, chemical dread.
Because this is spring, the whole world under
a tourmaline sway, and the gates of the Cross
Bones cemetery, wanton with ribbons. We
will honour you, in that famished hour when
sorrow files its weasel teeth, and under
the wan spin of stars, in the unquiet sci-fi
of a mind that makes a drowned world
of this dockland. Hush now, hush. The night
is the ambient temperature of a carsick sob,
and in the scrubby parkland the litter bins
are trying their very best to grow.

Devil

It was you all along: you dressed the dogs in restlessness,
and wheresoever your kisses land, the acne gathers. The TV
is thick with Americans, talking their awkward astronaut's
English. Donald is busy: stunned pussy, Home Alone cameo.
Bathrooms are cold spider-bounty. Fat white tonsils of mistletoe,
a sudden rash on the back of my hand. The sauce thickens,
opinions skew, fire begins to climb the curtain. I recognise your
detrimental handiwork: Miranda Hart and Kirstie Allsopp, a lispy
carol sung at half the speed of blowing glass. You wait for
the cover of darkness, then slide the stones back into their fruits.
Trust nothing. The limp handshakes of overcooked veg, and every
third thin Eat Me date is a catshit in disguise. I am not fooled.
Yours is the Kingdom of the ice-cream headache, the acid
heartburn, the hat that didn't suit. A whole family drowned in
their car in County Kerry. The big unlucks and small. Nothing is
too much trouble for you: stag dissolved in headlights, the mirage
before impact, the smug brat in the iPad ad, a round uncharted
apple, suddenly bad in the bowl.

On weekends

I might not wash today. I might
let the weekend slide into gratifying
anarchy. I am supposed to be thankful,
this town is not among the true nightmare
portions of the world. A roof over my head
and quite sufficient shine on the silver,
thanks. I might, though. Haven't you seen it?
Your city pokes a crafty fang at a flight path.
It's my city too, I suppose. You think you
are in control. Idiot! To name is to own, not
to know. And now we are so used to blood we
miss the silly crimson pity of it. I dream of
hardmen, the torturer's tweezers; of scholars
supplanting their teeth in basement gardens.
It's there, but you miss it. I don't miss
a thing. It's always there, the aura before
a seizure, inside my expendable circuitry,
deeper than dog years down, always, even
always. I dream of the made face coming
apart in my hands like wet bread. I might not
dress today. I might suck sauce from the bottle.
Here's mud in your *gloria mundi*, and a blue
blowtorch to your extremities, dear. How do
you feel about that? Or the massive enigma
of love? Does anything shock you? I
am supposed to be grateful, the shirt on
my back and quite enough coal in the cellar,
thanks. But the grand mal growls at the back
of the mind, and the back of the mind is
a bottle bank, love. We come and go, stooped
in their palisades. The rich are always with us,
their hexentanz and agonies. Here's Kate, we all
love Kate, oblivious, bombshell, and didn't
she used to be us? Not me. Your city, its nicotine
fingers, windows lit, yellow and sickly. Here we
crouch with our snouts to the damp plaster. I might
not leave the house today. Haven't you seen what's
out there? Their vaunting faith; the awful punitive
spring. I dream of muti and suitcases; grown men
stabbed in their Camden hamlets, eyes without
faces, world without end. It's there, still there,
but you do not see it. I see everything. I see it all.
And the Billy-born-drunks in the house next
door are shouting again. Inadmissible figments
slurred through the wall.

Dazzler

'Like diamonds we are cut by our own dust.' — *The Duchess of Malfi*

No, not a duchess, whose nature is a dance of iridescing,
but a pallid aspie with a smoker's cough. I sit in the kitchen
for hours at a time, compete with the fruit in the fruit bowl
at withering, or lean into my mirror, unable to decide
between *ravaged* or *effaced*. My lips are so red and so sharp
they could kiss the skin off a cold peach. But whores pout,
ladies frown. I pixelate myself with pearl dust, coax my skin
to a flat gleam. Nighttime is a paregoric lozenge. I am stately.
I am waiting for all the tricks you'll try to send me mad.

Where is my child? I held him as he slept, pink in twitching
time-lapse like footage of a flower. A moment only. To fill
the days I learn the words to Lili Marlène and sing it out of
the side of my mouth. I refuse to eat, and my Karen Millen
maxi dress enfolds me like a fumigation tent. Where is my son?
And where is his father? In the bathroom my scalloped nudity
takes an age to upload. I am tired. I must move slowly, stand
with my heels together, corrode and fold into souk blue shadow.
My legs don't work, won't run. Prognosis: mermaid.

Turn the radio on, heel and toe and howling. But no, I am
Nobody's *loony*, not yet. Open the window, let London's
smoky starfield strain its light through my upturned face.
Breathe out my Benzos and Bensons. I am nodding the sky
inside of me. I will make my world in the air. My world,
not this dingy Margaritaville of bland godliness. My world
is danced not lived, head thrown back and vaulting a roar.
My world is where my fingers married up and down his tattooed
back, false nails walking a roseate rain.

Not a duchess, but a scheme of gowns and tapers.
A *lady* is something planned like a heist. A *lady*
is a conspiracy, whispered up by brothers. I must
parcel my hands, demure at fist and flute. I have gone
inside. I tell myself I am still myself, that I will kick
more than I scream, and rather my scissors pretend
to some indiscriminate vein than this. But I wasn't born
for sweeping gestures. I shall buff my face to solid shine
and cut the hands I pass through.

Some small beseeching

Come darkness, my meticulous apothecary, and make
more liquid. Do not restage some swaggering hurt, but
soothe the shapes of solid objects. I can cry no more.
Arrest our brittle labours, conjugate the colour blue. You
honey suffering so, and I would sleep. My face invites
a veil, but I refuse. And I told you before, that I can cry
no more. I've scraped the mourning from the toast, I've
plumbed the day's unsolvable extent, and leant against
grief's fussy art for aid to no advantage. Unmake the bed
I've lain in, please. I've come to hate the hospitals:
a nurse with lipstick on her teeth, the sucked in guts
of injured pride, discrete catastrophe. I cannot cry, I said.
I'm not afraid of death, hygienic adversary with the self-
effacing smile. His breath is arak, acetone, erodes
the stone I stand on. I am *not* afraid. He schleps my
splendored guilts in his sample case, all swatches
and bottles; his handshake an affected palsy. *He's*
afraid of *me*. But come, darkness. My head is surrounded:
immoderate swallows whose sharpened beaks will seek
to break a vein. I am *so* tired, so sick of either ritual or
physic, anything you'd throw to dogs. I would sleep.
Your deafness is a remedy. I will not dream, to see him
rising like a phoenix out of seizure. I will apply myself
to blindness. I'll scorn the glitchy fates that say there's
meaning here, or reason. I'll spurn Atropos first, an
alkaloidal siren, shit-faced at a ribbon cutting. *Bitch, put
down your scissors or you're going to get hurt.* Come
dark, no more of this. Or illness' quotidian perfume,
the fevered sheets of invalids, the prematurely wept.
I cannot cry. I won't. But I will be the broom with which
the beach is swept. The sea will cover everything. A salt
estate that makes a nonsense of denial.

On insomnia

And contemplate this: the heat-treated hairdos of next door
neighbours, the roseate nosebleeds of fuckboys in hoodies;
your own face, rinsed in the mirror, the sweet green sweat
you're riddled with in mornings, a rock pool reflection under
algaecidal light. You are going nowhere. This poem yokes
you, to the pain you are chronic and adipose with; to the desk,
to the chair, to ergonomic purgatory. And to the body, its
spasms and its rhapsodies, three part harmonies, one chord
wonders. *You will never be whole.* The voices. His voice,
broadcast on your remedial frequency, making its way
through a rubbishy dusk, the streetlamps beaming fizzy glow
like Lucozade. You will never be whole. Vomit o'clock
and the brain is Kraken, white and shaking. Open the window,
pry the chipboard from the window; fill your punctured eye
with stars. And contemplate this: Saturday night and the dirt
purrs with it; cars, litter bins, pit bull dogs. A girl with high
Yorick cheekbones drags a false nail down the scratchy
surface of a bri-nylon sleeplessness. A man rides ignorance
like a white horse, kicking mirrors from parked cars. You
have the itch under your skin. Insectile dysfunction. Lust,
with its own murky gravities. *You will fail.* You have not
made a friend of this city and *you will fail.* Cup your eyes
like coins. Addiction holds such simplicity. Check your
used-car contours in the broken glass. You are going
nowhere. They cannot nail you to a pronoun, hot mess
of cravings and behaviours, tainted frailty, old meat's
rancid rainbow. Ugly. Contemplate. Consider: your
lilies, toiling like deaf ears, tearing the tired night a new
one, stirring a sulphate dust in your veins. Your eyes
are blue with pseudo-scientific toxicity, with chemical
expectancy, a dread that dries a smile like paint. Your
blood is on fire, full of bellicose adrenaline, nitrate
and neon; brighter, even, than the hoary fluorescence
of angels. It is so late. And you are pining the rhinestone
shine of a lost narcotism. Now trauma's your ergotamine.
Trauma, your ergot, your argot of rye. Awful thought
that treads the brain's rank breadth. Silence. Pray silence.
Pray the dark room away, the candles, the pious vibrations
of flame; the dim bulb with its gospel of moths, one
hundred pairs of gloved hands clasped to powder.
Marooned in your gooseflesh, one hand does not know
what the other is doing. It's three a.m. the mind's alive

like frostbite, a cold burn that blackens things. Your graphite smile could shatter. Thoughts of him have poisoned you, rust in the blood. You have not eaten for days, you mottle, run your own hands over your oxidising thighs, watch the bruises ripen to a landmass, a landmark, a *brave new world*, a *here be dragons.* You listen to yourself, creaking like rope; your body, its canned laughter repeating mean and low, throwing out thought according to the malnourished algorithm some devil has devised. You clutch and sway in a crêpe air and you *want-want-want* what you'll never have again: sleep; his image breaking across your scrubbed flesh like surf. Contemplate this: this is forever. There is no movie montage where you'll shop yourself to transformation. You will never be whole. And grief is not a line we walk to wellness; the tidy smirk of therapy, the therapised, the girls licking flakes of gold leaf pastry from a Pret a Manger croissant, saying *you should take up yoga.* Grief is a longing in the body, your body, the machine-tooled aesthetics of starvation. It's so uncool, a super-terrestrial emptiness; the acetone eroded teeth of your disorder. He will not come again. Sleep will not come, and make an amnesty of bandages, the white ribbons rendering you prematurely maypole. It will not wrap you. It will not keep you. It will not launder or succour you. It will break into your ballerina box, will chew the jewels from their semi-precious sockets, set them pulsing in your frontal lobe. Your heart has a headache. Drink raw egg. Or Dettol. It's up to you. The sky is pasteurised by thunder…

Giallo

I was made for tantrum and for schnapps, for tenebrated
nakedness, libidinous guignol. You might not think so,
but it's true. Pamper the hatchet, play for me those three
black keys in a scorpion chord. I'll wear the reddest dress
in recorded history. Cut me from my stockings with
teary-eyed and tomfool scissors. Your love lives in your
left hand, baby. In a pretty smile. In a string of pearls.
A sting of pearls. I was made for all the gargoyle vices
of men. My hair is loose, and gross with roses. Lush wet
fault I'm sweating with. Heavy breath, queenly spite. I was
made for this. My vinegar contrition, twisted seam in
American nylon. I'm a difficult word in your runny mouth.
Crack the spine of hymnals in a church. I'm here in a bad
habit, baby, in diamonds as big as babies' heads. I am wiles
and foibles, delirious in yellow light. Take me on the sawdust
floor of a circus tent. Jagged pout you'd target for a trophy,
the smile in woozy splinters, rearing teeth. You might not
think so, but it's true. Sumptuous in punishment; embellishing
a death with leather and lapis. Suave with discontent. *Bella
figura.* Arrive at a typecast ecstasy. There is a ruby moon
tonight. There is a bead upon a needle, an angel raving
on the head of a pin, pricked and teased and pleasing
to God, laid out on the bed like a body in the library.
I'm made for this. Believe me now? I shiver like a table
at a séance. Put your hands on me. Your housebreaker's
gloves. Recidivist kink I buck and sway with. Ply my snide
arousal like a pro. A blonde wig and a change of clothes.
I'm tendering kinetics for a dare. Delicious risk I run and bleat
with. Wrap me in a red screen, in a bed sheet, in a pair of Mae
West lips. Treat my jaundiced bones with bleach. Oh, I was
born for all of this.

Gentleman Caller

The Cavan night aspires to knives; a dog with a prominent
spine is moving among the empties like a broken plough. I
am alone, and the wet, electric air is humming. My boys is
gone to town, to pander the black keys of a rival smile; to
knead their queasy music from the local *faces*. This feud
is what men do; old women wait with the tattered sacks
of onions, sagged beside a dying fire. And so I sit, in my
flickering kitchen fiefdom, where green potatoes trail their
whitish roots like comets, else shrink in silver blankets,
sputtering, dribbling victims of shock. I sit and I rock,
coddle our cuts of meat like a midwife, madwife – rabbits
plump and dead and sleek. I caresses them, lost in thought,
jugged in the wine-dark juice of a rash winter. I sippet my
sauce. I suck at a fat cheroot. I wipe my nicotine fingers
on the jaggy back of a whelping bitch. I am waiting. I am
alone, and this is *his* time, my time, and *he* will come,
and I will come, back to myself from a black hole deep
as poacher's pocket. I watch our starveling Tom steering
his long shadow between the table legs. I smile. I was
a young girl once and moved like a cat's shadow. I was
a young girl once, my smitten kiss would sting like snow.
I was young, and *he* was young, and we were young in
our loitering love. They called me *fox*, for the teaseled
burlesque of my redbrown hair. They called him *bear*,
he carried a razorblade under his nail. I remember well,
the smell of hay, our shivering tryst behind the burnt-out
barn; the way he held my wrist, his fist as tight as a wet
knot. I was cold white feet, in a sateen slip. I danced
delight into his amber eyes, my body a tactical sapling,
oh, the slumberous shockwaves of me! *He* was in my
brain, my blood, like spring's green treatment. When I
was young. I am alone. I wait. The night sky spits
and flashes like a damp electric fence. My boys is gone
to town, and God, how my old bones saw at themselves.
This feud is what men do, their women wait, have waited.
I have always waited; gas down low to amplify his
staggered light, I watch across the stunted field. Or
venture the hedges in summertime. Or tend to a gash
in the earth's green yield.

And I will consider the yellow dog

After Christopher Smart

And Smart saw God concentric in his cat.
Smart's cat, artificing faith from cyclone
volition. There is no God in you, yellow
dog. Your breath is our daily quicksand;
you juggle your legs into an avid heap.
You are bent on death. There is no God
in you. You are imperfect and critterly.
I *will* consider you, for all of that. Today,
as you joust farewell to the park; the pack
in their garrison palsy, tails agog, and you,
cocking your head to cup Madam's strewn
bark, your nose like an antique brooch
in the sun. I will consider you, yellow dog,
as you twist in a rapt mechanical dream.
I will consider your coat, the colour
of fenced gold; how you are your own
secular halo. I will consider your skull,
the narrow skull of a young gazelle
whose victory is leaping. And I will
consider your eyes, their hazel light
a gulp of fire, those firewater eyes,
holding now a numb depth down,
and milkier flickering monthly. I will
consider your youth, when we didn't
know if you would saunter or quake;
when we didn't know if you
would prove savvy or giddy or both.
It was both. Our frank amaze at your hardy
smarts! Our silly delight at each degree
of more-than-human knowing. I will
consider you, yellow dog, your pale
moods and your gazing; your fidgets
and your snoozes. There is no God in you,
the deep-time of a dog year is enough.
And lately you are wiser than all zero.
Dear dog, creaking like a haunted house,
I will consider you, from bucking *young*
'un to patient as settling porter; how you
held the pack when Fat Man was small
and a zoomy nuisance of wriggling. I will

consider the soft hum of you, aslant against
my chest in grief, in grieving, overwhelmed,
when you were the busy broom that swept
the pieces of me together. Yes, I will
consider the yellow dog, his bestowing
snout in the chill AM; his royal cheek
and his dances. A yellow dog comes only
once and is hisself: brilliant, final and entire.

A ghost in our house

Not you, but your after-image. A taste
in my mouth like waking parched, when
need has a weight and a flavour.

Nobody knew *what to do* with you. Mine
is a slippery pain that will not settle, that
questions and fidgets, just like a child.

I do not want to sleep. The dusty room
gathers its looming symmetries. Memory
squats, befouling the shadows, tearing
the legs off spiders.

I don't know why. But I do know this:
*when you've been hungry then nothing
is ever enough.*

Hunger remembers, hunger records,
like tape, like stone. In the dark our
hungers mushroom, become a fungus
in the lung.

Impeded breath and panic comes.
Our most resonant malady, brightest
light, distorted sound and soft. *We*
knew this thing, just me and you.
Some truths cannot be held.

The nightworld has no need for words,
it does not seek to name the shapes
it strands like sighing islands in the bed,
the corners, boxes, stacks.

Times I feel *I* might forget, but love
restores what language lacks, and I
am not alone.

Save for this particular, self-
important loss, a strutting silence
in the head. Gnawer of the living
bone.

My friend I eat the hours. You have
gone where talk will not return you.

At the upmost top of the stairs on
the landing, what's left of you is standing
          like a darker patch of dark.

'Daddy', indeed

After Sylvia Plath

A male muse should remain buried.
You rise like a red velvet curtain. You
rise to thread that fat part of your smile
through a curved hook. Your smile, most
unmentionable worm. Brocade of skin.
Your mouth has been a shrine I fringe
with fire, or feed with coal. There's smoke
enough to swell a chimney. You are not
dead. The wardrobe isn't closed, and no
cold shirts yearn for you. I am milking
my long fingers. I take off my gloves
with my teeth. My fingers concentrate
their venom, my poison pursuing
a suitable stream. I have no name for
you. There is no name to stitch its label
to your stiff lapel. Nor shall I compare
you. Oh, the world is old enough to make
a harvest of such fathers, and you are
the size of your own modest crippling.
No less, no more. A male muse should
remain among the inveterate-earthed
with mud under his tongue. You rise
to retrieve your fist from the wall.
Your body is soft. You sustained
your softness like an injury. You have
no discipline. You have pinned your
discipline to your children. To the Irish.
To your Irish child. To your Mormon Christ.
To an image of yourself as most robustly
victimised. To an image of yourself
as Christ's child. But when you kneel,
your own weight pushes you into the earth
and I am glad. I have no name for you.
There is no name. And I am nameless.
Stay down. You will not rise to ring
my skinny wrist, banded and scarred
like the leg of a pigeon. One more
time.

Dear Comrade

London skies are graphite and aggrieved. Here, patrician
chimneys, an ambulance's blue disquiet; sparrows, flags,
a turbulence of starlings. Days we cannot coax our own
bent luck to breathe; no time for bliss or frill, for feeding
pigeons from the windowsill. On days like these fate finds
us peevish, lame, and destined for some penance. Or
for coffee's unprincipled liquorice spree. Our tongues
will turn the loamy earth like spades. We know where to
go: away from all the wet brains running their frictionless
mouths; the carbon-neutral haircuts, declaiming their cold
idea. Ours is an afternoon's bruised republic: a creaking
stair, the crooning French, a semi-coherence of weather,
words. Where poems come, these cannibal colossi, eat
the flesh that falls from me. Art, in carnivorous mufti, puts
out a pristine polar light, as finite as a trial. To remain at
large, and undevoured: this is a skill that's practiced by few.
To name but two, the girl for whom all smiles are storms;
Saint Icarus as astronaut. By which is meant both me and you.
Laugh. To ricochet round galleries, fugitive, uncivilised;
to aim an erring joy, to walk, to seek, to find, at least to feel.
And underneath the fumbled iridescence of a yellow lamp
invent the crooked, reckless real. London skies emphatic
with fractional glare. Where a grass verge is sentenced
to dogs, where the moon is a hooked finger, where the moon
hangs pendant and suggestible, pure as a virgin's earring,
pure as a Medici pearl. We do not see the world the way they do,
want parables and tangerines; velvet lapels, the gold auratic
swell of holy things. To ask *why not?* To push our luck down
alleyways abandoned to their infamy, and saloon bars beneath
a chandelier's prodigious silly crystalline. To want the world,
in short, entire, and make the asking plush. Sweet to an unfixed
occasion of flowers. To lean into adventure in second-hand
shoes. To embrace the doleful spectrum, the fallible and riotous
too. Though sometimes we might sit in squinting phobic
at the news, we rise again: wayward, Lazarian, to meet
the future anywhere with thirst. God save us,
from the petty spiral of hindsight; from forgetting
under London skies, to count out each shivering,
ostracised star.

True Confessions of a Catholic Schoolgirl

For Charlene

Friday night is viral blight, the monitor glowing with gilded intensity.
Here is a mirthless acre of flesh; sex is the shivery pain you roar and cramp
with. Now you are sliding right. I tell you, *you can Google me.* I disclose
myself in parts: gingham, pleats, and long white socks, my father's massive
bicep wearing black. *What is it you think you know about me?* Mine is a mood
you might take tweezers to; my mood resisting spring's green peek-a-boo,
with cats alive in the redolent hedges. Despair's a kind of clockwork lust.
Technician to your winding up. *What is it you think you know about me?*
Winter isn't shrugged, my dear, not round here, and you want something,
*every*thing: the giddy habit of my lust, the truth, the meme, the myth.
But honesty's the lowest form of impotence. Inside is a thundery hurt,
it's been this way for years. I am wakeful and genderless. *You* ask all
the wrong questions. *I* never learnt to separate my *grievance* from my *grief.*
I spent a life in trying to keep my clotted wrists above the waterline. *Hail
Mary* in the fraying dusk. I say the shrapnel in my flat, broad bones.
This is *not* a metaphor. I say *it's easy to be brave when someone loves you.*
How do you make a study of forgetfulness? A hobby out of loss? The silence
thickens. The silence is like fur, it strokes one way. You brush against it. I say
stop giving *compliments*; *stop* taking *photos.* If you could feel how I feel. If it
was your unyielding guilt that scribbled things in notebooks. I've no right to
be alive. I swelter in a white shirt. The climate grinds. Everyone avoids me.
I'm as cynical as science. I will not be improved upon, or fumbled with,
like women are, *real* women. You don't know how to talk to me, trope
faith you make a fetish of. No, I did not *keep the uniform.* In the air behind
me the saints are perfecting their deaths, screwing them into my brain
like lightbulbs.

The Miracle of the Rose

I want you to buy me a rose so perfect
it is a logo of a rose.

I see that this statement surprises you.
I see you arranging your face
in undecided Clip Art, not quite sure
whether to smile or not. But lover,
I am deadly serious. I want a rose and I
can be *such* a girl at times, concocting
fanciful agonies, mixing a bad mood
like an alkaloidal daiquirí.

Where is my rose? That is not my rose.
These are not my roses, not real roses, wrapped
in plastic pinafores like pauper lunatics. God!
Send me a redolent spoof of a rose. I am ripe
with the horny grief of growing, and I demand
a craving rose, a rose like a smacked gob, a splashy
gallop of roses.

Did you not know that love is laundered
through roses like money is laundered
through banks? You'd better bring me a rose,
an inoperable rose, a rose whose red can only
mean emergency. I want the torn curse of a rose,
a debauch of thorns, the deep archaic spite of a rose.

A rose, or you do not love me. A prowl of roses,
the gouge of a rose, a scarlet pyre of preening petals.
Or what, I am for long-faced lilies only? For tulips
as white as a near-death experience? Flowers that are
figurines of flowers? A pursed bud like the frowning
mouth of a mother in-law?

Talk to me. Give me an insult of roses,
blackened roses, dead as spent fireworks.
Better yet, steal for me the moist slow-motion
of a rose, new rose, opening, like an infant's
sudden fist.

Epistle from inside the Sharknado

You might call it *God*; might witness the weather's
disjointed volition, and figure it biblical payback
for all your long decades of self-defeating industry:
the gasses in the atmosphere, the poison in the water.
And you might stand on your lawn in your shorts,
running a scream up a flagpole; sniffing catastrophe's
rank surfeit on the bilious air. You might, for all I
know. For all I care you could be crouching in
rainy basements, debating *plague* or *commies* with
the cans of beans; courting immortality with *forward
planning* until your lungs fill up with sand like canvas
punching bags. It means nothing to me, the human
world: humourless delinquencies, the corkscrew
politics of plunder and of blame; *victims* of this or
that, rolling a moistened eye to camera. I see you,
surrounded by dripping debris, in the local anchor's
sallow limelight, *angling* and righteous. *Nuke
the sharks!* It will not save you. I will come again.
We will come, seismic and genderless, thick sleeves
of meat, working the humid air like a grudge. You'd
better run. You'd better equip yourself with guns,
and chainsaws, consult a TV psychic, burn your
money, shave your head, sell your kids, anything at
all. I am coming round again. *We* are coming,
driven by insomnia's deficient logics, our no-
escape velocity. You will know us by the shine
of our endangered Kevlar; my exoskeletal corset
rips your fingers into kelp. You might call it *God*,
but it's not *God*. The sky is singing with Nature's
maniac gusto. It's the only game in town. Come,
hurtle over the swooning horizon, stare into my
flat-screen eye, and tell me, human, it is not so.

Happiness

Is the one thing that *tastes as good as skinny feels.* Or, for me at least, the paschal stink of churches; is beauty as a Byzantine rite. It is the mournful swagger of an aisling, old men singing with haunted gusto, and M's tattoo of asphodels, the winter sun, set sweet and low. And also Bucovina, the days we stood inhaling yellow rain, a skyline bandaged with factories. It is the green air you live to taste but once. Tomcats and car horns, exhaustive refrain, and your laugh, spangled by a hangover, the night we played Ouija, when the glass abandoned its alphabet, went whizzing at the wall. I wasn't always fond, have wanted to be numb, and known the suckling pride of addicts. I have banded with a wastrel tribe, coercing a dull bliss from grief's malarial quotidian. Grief was bloody breakneck, then, sparing no horses and flanked by bats, approaching at an anxious gallop. Grief, the debauched brainchild of rock 'n' roll suicides; the sheepish creed of fathers, the vast alarm of nations. Sad gluttony of spirit, grief. Everything that kills you in the end. But happiness. That's love's low wattage on a leafy day. That's impulse buying black sateen. That's holy as a horse fair, kiddo; the shallow cup where kindness kernels, spreading like some friendly germ.

'Drinks with friends'

An estate pub is the only place left to tolerate
her doused yearning. Tonight, when she returns
her proofed face from the ladies, no one will know
she's been praying, no one will know she is wearing
faith, meagre as a red leather mini-skirt; no one
will know that she was singing into the broken
soap dispensers: *God, whisk me to a winning streak.*
Take me where everything is one hit wonderful, and I
don't have to bite back all the shit I'm rotten with!

An estate pub is the last place she can go
to transform crack-up into antics, and when
she locks herself into the end cubicle, she is
kneeling, not crouching, fudging a novena
with Bacardi breath. And when she stands
in the middle of the room, in the way
like a three-legged stool, no one is struck
dumb by her baby blues, nor her Winehouse
hair, nor her tallowy arms. She is unwoman.
A nun.

An estate pub is her just reward. She will join
the Real Housewives, free-styling their petty
betrayals; the karaoke knock-offs syncing *Theme*
from a State of Blank Frenzy, over and over. One
among many top-heavy girls, nodding like foxgloves,
crooked on shots. And no one will know that she
has been praying. God is sieved through drink,
her thoughts are chemical plankton, phosphorescing,
strobing, sifted, drifting, gone.

Here is a bottle of House Red, a little lizard
on the label. Here is yellow tequila, glowing
in votive rows. Here is the gilded Papal slug
of Goldschläger, its slick cowlicks of fire
dancing in her head. Here is her face,
flat and grubby as a used nicotine patch.
And here is her stung knuckle, a reliquary,
gnawed white.

On trauma

The bedroom varies its light. Far bleak of day, I blank.
I can't. Outside is moods and male sweating. Some pour
love through funnels of flesh. I hate the steep handiwork
of towns, where cretins bask in their fetishes. It's morning
now, my teeth heave. Vomit. Dysmorphic trembling.
My legs have not seen sunlight since nineteen ninety-five.
And here is the news, a yellow eye that roves the reveal
and waits for blood. There's always one. The scurried
burlesque of suburbia, preternatural nets atwitch for
the kid who *kept to himself,* his melon-head pranked
open: unpopular, ginger, and *they didn't mean it.* Uh-
huh. A moral crusade is a tune you can hum. Here's
May, the draconian melee, their idiot intention. Farrow,
his seismic face shook into rubble and politic. The super-
rich: Kate, and Zara, and Beatrice, cartoon and vestal.
Goddesses all, both bountiful and damned. Ground Zero
is a patient feedback form that says *I couldn't, the mask
had swallowed my face.* A mind that traffics in tigers,
yeah? No, there is no legislating for an idiot. And leave
me alone with the clucked deadpan of my own voice.
This sickness comes to moderate my content. A bumper
fist in the mirror. I spike my errand. I give up the day.
A pill, and my gums glow Tyrian. I'm lit like a glass
house gathers its light, like a glass house sucking in
stones. *I did not understand the question.* Taunting
the gormy boxes with ticks. This town is full
of diseases, conditional fucks, walking cultures. I saw
them, bacteriologically smitten, palming a face with
a face at a bus stop.

Come home

For a chance to attend to the changing light, to have
done with the world and its limitless severing, once
and only once, walk out. There is green beneath
the hangnail of the world, if you would look. Deer
with dynastic faces, turned away in profile, and life
applies itself thickly to the hedgerows. Put as much
of the sky as you can behind you. The rabbits, breeding
like bad ideas, an owl inventing deafness, skinny foxes
crouching in the costume of their cunning. These things
do not belong to you. To you alone the light. To you,
alone, worrying some customary grievance. You didn't
know how hungry you were until your spade struck
bone, turned over your own face. Behold: the skull
exhibits its cracked-spinel eye! The earth will not
pander to preciousness. The earth swallows everything.
Witness to a silhouette, a running dog, a sharp black
bough you'd break across your knee. Bloodless lips
reflected in the cleansed palates of puddles. Your
family unfolding in the curve of your jaw.
Everything. This home will suck the secrets from
your fingers. The wedding rings of the dead. The light
belongs to you alone. To you, alone. Toads are decently
cupped in their burrows. The sheep's brain swims in
its suspect jelly. A fistulated cow is a window on
the world. And pheasants, plumply martyred are
like farmers' daughters murdered in their beds.

Rock bottom

He walked out over the estuary, like King
Cnut contradicting the tide. He walked until
the numb pearlescent light spread from his
waist like a grey soutane. The gulls rose up
around him, startled and horny as sailors on
shore leave, alarmed by the possible sky,
its cold miraculous lack. He walked with
his hands at his sides, his white cuffs
trailing like paper boats. He walked until
his fingers pushed deep into the creamy
haunches of a wave. He walked until
freezing water ate holes through his best
black jacket like moths, till it smoothed
the creases from his shirt; till it twisted
his tie like a charmed snake. He stepped
into vanishing, knelt without solemnity
or fervour, was met by a velvety purring
dark. And this is how I picture him,
marbled, cosseted and drowsing, on a bed
of blue anemones. His smile a lustring
relic, eyes like sunken stars.

On guillotines

Monday is wrongness with knobs on. I cling
to the dog like I'm lashed to a mast. My friend
asks what I'm afraid of. What am I afraid of?
The woman next door, her Mersey perm; men
in general, ridicule and malnutrition. All of it,
really. Everything. I'm afraid of being arrested,
detained without charge, of blowing my phone
call. Afraid for my friends, the North, the revels
we pretend to. Afraid of trying too hard. Afraid,
just afraid. Monday. The sun goes up and down
like a bus on its tired hydraulics. I go up
and down, though mainly down. Afternoons, I
throw my solitude at the wall in strings, it sticks
like cooked spaghetti. Turn on the TV, absorb
its distortion. On RT there's a child, his chest
is slowly filling up with air. He inflates himself
like a blood pressure cuff; he's brown and bones
as a peat bog sacrifice. Make another cup of tea.
Someone somewhere is having it worse. *Don't
cry for me, Ballymena!* Everyone laugh at the funny
joke. But I am still afraid. We're all afraid, our fear
tickles the strip-lights, spreads like a cough in a cinema.
Monday. I hoovered the rug in front of the shrine
for the first time in months. I could lose the plot
and spiral to Christ, his all-consuming love, his totally
tedious chivalry. He wants my soul in the same
way the farmer wants a dog. His *ee-i-ad-i-oh* banging
a gong in my knotty gourd. I could lose the plot. But
mine is a sapling madness, bends and does not break.
My faith keeps luck on a key chain; counts out
the magpies on fingers. Monday. I'm stuck on fear
like a ballgown in the branches. The mind stalls at it,
a zip stiff half way to fastened. What am I afraid of?
Serenity, the mouths in which the butter melts. A strap
to my back; the ease of kneeling. Peers of the Realm,
their padlocked luck, their lack of a clue, their big
ideas: they're coming for me. After that they'll be
coming for you.

Children of the Night

I'm hungry and I can taste hairspray, there's smoke in the bedroom;
a black light blunders against the brain. House cats carry their tails
like sceptres, think they are better than us; they are probably right, in
and out as they like, slutting around in narrow bands of purple shadow.
I finger my playlist louder; bite down on a payload of miniature bliss,
sugar steeped in sweet hibiscus 'sinthe. *Apéritif*, I let it rock and fold
me. There's a boy in the bed and he's talking again; his words eat
holes in my longing like dogs: *ooh, baby*, he says. I close my eyes.
His blood is a shuddering phosphate cocktail: ptomaine, cocaine's
tinfoil toothache. I can smell it. He's sweating his snakebite; his lips
don't move in sync. Young Puck, deadbeat and liable to spike or
wilt. Whoreson, savant, *punk as fuck*. I lie as still as flat lemonade.
I can be patient. I am drifting in and out, listening to traffic, to tomcats
and foxes; the cocksure stereophonics of cars. My city slurs in her
splitfoot slang. Camden, a dithering grammar of knives; repertoire
of wounds and juices. I am at home here, my hunger is at home. I
chew my tongue. He's looming again, blue gummed and smudgy-
goth, Grimaldi with emetic mouth, black lipstick on, and such is
life: a dull, rank, baffled mess of statutory discord. Weekends are
worst, *the* worst, a hotwire in the head, and *eff all* on the telly. So
it's this or else sit in, doing my chemical penance from *rise and shine*
to *roll credits*, backcombing my hair and climbing the walls, because
I am hungry. My hunger comes and bites my living daylights out, so
strong it makes a blood sport of my senses. I pick him up in clubland,
flaunted and scoring; beckon him back with a breath that smells
of wet cement; with a breath that smells of spent matches, ethanol
and atropine. He doesn't notice, and I must feed, skimpily fetish
in leather and lace. Gorgeous short-changeling, *up fer it*. I can
taste hairspray, aftershave and high alarm. I run my tongue
across my teeth, and test his fine raised veins like braille. He falls
back, acutely climaxed, shipwrecked on a daybed, preened in his
own mildewed pearls. His eyes are wide, his skin is cold. I roll
him over, wipe my mouth along my sleeve. Blood's red pheromone
loose in the room. My dress is Gideon Bible Black. I belong to this
place. Forever, amen.

Contains mild peril

i

The bad book opened up in sad placating palmistry. Today my face is a charm school of partial eclipse. Today I will wear my Moretta [a *dumb mask* you hold in place with your teeth]. Silence is pleasing, both to husbands and to God. This is not poetry. Today the face fancies itself as a hole. Before I put on my Moretta I will chew ritual sweetvetch and get up my hair into flowering ramparts. I am a prodigy of sexploitation and female-specific pain. I am black lace and brute bootyliciousness. I am *giallo*, my death is a popularity contest. This mask is for use in emergencies only.

ii

Wednesday's Child is sputtering out her permafrosted consonants. Today I am thin Lizzy Siddal. I put on my Dama, and then I am stark and raving. This mask deals in absolutes. Pretentious moi is a red head, an orthodox whore with a starry crush of penetrative pronouns. Pretentious moi has ninety-nine names, is drenched in her own extrovert suppleness, pale and protein-free in party clothes. This is not poetry. Bitch is a bathtub Ophelia in her no frills wickedness, a thrift of flowers. Bitch is a bindweed bombshell, crass as a Poor Clare, utterly ignorant, porous with mercy. This mask is *all things to all men*. It weights the face like your heaviest thought.

iii

This is every record that ever made you want to slit your wrists and then some. I am a rendition Madonna, a spectacle of bio-luminescent virginity. No, I am a Medusa, perspiring and saliva and every word mistakes a snake. No, I am Ian fucking Curtis, an analogue Lorca singing the blues. No, my whole head is a sad Calaca stiff with marigolds. Yes, my mask is a louche señora, bright with rude hauteur, ideal for when the jaw clamps shut like a music box and all speech is self-harm. My mask is a mask for when you are dead. My mask is a mask for when your fingers refuse the piano. My mask is hardnosed, mechanically explicit, absolutely tasteless. A mask to mean my short-lived lusts, sealing my face shut like an evidence bag.

iv

I am Caliban and there is no mask just a life that I wear like a bag on my head. Minotaur, whose thoughts are jutting horns, whose long face is its own scold's bridle. When I am Caliban spirits of the air surround me like wasps around a litter bin. Girl as a grimacing fakir, anorexic and pig-headed with penitence. When I am Caliban I am wider than flood defences with *nobody loves me*. I eat worms. I comb the crackbaby tangles from my beehive hair and pioneer new stress positions, squatting under bridges. When I am Caliban I am too ugly for even sunlight. My face should be shut up in an attic. My face is a speaking clock. My face is a fifteen certificate.

A tiny band of glittering stones

I am wearing the bracelet I found while cleaning the cottage,
my wrist an irregular yellow brick road. I have stood for an hour
and stared at the garden, ranking your cats in order of shifting
wildness, one by one, with dust on the seat of my jeans. My nails
are black, and I am wearing the bracelet I found while cleaning
the cottage. I tell myself you *wouldn't mind* that I'd enlist
the careful flattish shine of gems, a preciousness I can't invent,
can only ever borrow, so. Helps me feel less like myself. This
morning I've sorted your photos of you. Your knuckles nurtured
diamonds. When *you* were young the graspy limelight buoyed
you. Yours was tilt, and fad, and spree; savvy ingots, high-heeled
shoes, fashion's strutting tumult. Mine has been the bitten lip,
the free school meal, the dawning of a navy bruise. I am wearing
the bracelet I found while cleaning the cottage. I've worked until
the sweat stands cold along my spine. I've stuffed your clothes all
tight and angry fistfuls into sacks that split and squeak. The self
sinks into the self, a pearl dissolving in a glass of wine. I boxed
your books. I lay your letters flat. I opened drawers and let my hands
go wincing over trinkets: tangled skeins, and gilded shrapnel, baby
teeth. I cut my thumb. I found a family Bible, whitish-gold on black,
the raised typography of scars. I separated scarves, washed bottles
of their quarter inch of curdled fire. I scrubbed the floor, and stood,
and stared, and counted cats. I am wearing the bracelet I found
while cleaning the cottage. I take it off. I tell myself *there is no
spell to break.* I'll give it back, and you. I snap the lid on
your rosewood box. My hair is swinging, stiff with dirt. I get
the light, I close the door. It won't stay shut. Eyes inside
the briar patch. The keys are lisping in their locks.

Valery in Zombieland

In aberrant October light an unexploded silence ticks within
the late café. You sway in your seat, sing under your breath,
courting a splintery shortwave; finessing the stilted fluorescence
of three a.m. *I hate this song.* We shrink inside of everything we
cannot say. *I love you*, for instance, not best but most. You're
egg and chips and typically shivering, forehead throbbed to
headache's mild telepathy; skin that lilac-blue beneath the same
old battered platinum aura, a staticky snowblind blonde I'd know
from merest flick of fringe. You can't sit still. I see your need
wash over you in steady waves like television. You must move,
and ask me will I walk with you, into these dank, inoperable
streets where Hawley's punters grunt their knuckle-sucking
music. It's raining, shattered glasses curry incandescence
on the pavement, the whole of Camden buzzing with a lairy
electricity. The Marathon's disbanded and staggered into
headlights, irregular and legless, they puke their rumbled guts.
Girls go by, tricked out for drunk dysphoric kabuki in
Islington clubs. You wince from this, head down, and edging
The Lock. I follow, till morning breaks, fissures into catalytic
stench and empty cans; the tidal smack of backed up drains,
carcinogens and stereos. I follow, disconsolate shadow, along
the canal, done out in dirty alloy, lapping at its plaquey banks.
The water reflects nothing, upholstered in cold poison. I follow,
picking the bones from your fractional stammer, your voice in
its low payphone acoustics, hollow at such an hour as this. We
drift, as Camden turns her leering derelictions to the tourists.
Aimless, underwhelmed, her sodden air gone green, gone blue,
Rastafarised. Dreadlocks selling one love lollies, preposterous
with THC. Anarcho-crust-patch vanguard on the bridge, old
friends we duck because you are *ashamed*, you say, and full
of squeamish guilt, that haunter of withdrawal. *Enough!* You
shrug and think how best to shake me. I hold your shoulders,
take you in, your combat boots and guttered cunning; your face,
upcycled silver mess as flickered in chill sunshine, October's
erring light. I let you go, you trail a weak green wattage through
the trees; retreat to mildewed alchemy, and numbly
conjured, disappear.

Gentry

The people round here have a used
look, as in these are the secrets I live
with, as in take your job and shove it.
Hand in carrier bag we are headed
for a coke-emboldened spring.
The girls wear impractical sandals.
And this is what you're entitled to.
And this is what you deserve. Didn't
you know, they are not the same thing?

It's too much sometimes. I don't
always look, but I know. And then,
the unyielded eye has cause to curse
the skull it swims in. No, I'm not
like you. That isn't to boast. On my
walk to work are cars crushed into
walls like faces buried in pillows.
And what are you holding in?
And what are you holding back?

Tell me again how full is life,
our haircuts and cuisine. Here
is a cat with a hookah tail.
Here are tattoos and childbirth;
other people's palsied photons
fastened to a screen. How full life
is; how infuriatingly miraculous.
Here is a pub quiz. Here is a play
list, the best of the nineties done
in streaky dulcet sleaze.

And where are you going? And where
are you from? The people round here
are chips with everything; stiff beef
on dry bread, recycled carbohydrates.
No, I am not like you, like them, some
third thing. The alky dark I shun; the club,
its terabytes of ecstasy. The people round
here are me / not me. That forklift face, the fouled
mouth, death and tracksuits, glandular animals.

And the briars on the waste ground are
lauding their thorns. Don't talk to me
about up and coming. Don't talk to me.
Don't talk.

Loneliness of the long distance runner

Here's the thing, to see Northern Ireland from a plane, caught
on this, the wettest day of the wettest year, somewhere between
reprisal and *amnesty*. Or, walking into a bar in the foetid West,
holding this tenebrated glass to my chapped lips, to whisper
another porous *slàinte* with my American cousins. To come
suddenly South in a thundery light, dragging the whole aphotic
squalor of my heart, demanding to be loved. To scale longing
in the lean and leaning East, the pushy purple hills rising
like selfish giants to meet me. To do all this, and still I do
not understand. To find that every door is shut. Aul' folks,
locked in a last prefab taboo, will send away a stranger-girl.
Here's the thing, to tug my ugly forelock to the graves, hushed
in drab esteem, to feel nothing at all for the longest time
among the shrines, the martyred kitsch, the rows of tea lights,
mouldy stone. For my guts to hurt, to enter the church bent
double, doing votive coaxing: *please to God and make it
good and I'll come good this one time once.* To bring you
flowers that stink of recession and petrol, to fumble with
frostbit fingers, kneeling at generic fences. To look for you,
and who I am, and how do I even begin to belong. To be
followed back on a Friday night to my Queen's Quarter
B&B by a ghost, to lean into his haunting as a driver on ice
turns into a skid. And what it is, is the sea is full of shadows,
and I am opening my phone, culling the numbers like rabbits.
It is to leave, resigned to being left. The thing is, living in
London, lapping the piss-pungent park in the morning, trying
to remember to breathe. The trick is to push myself harder,
to sweat you out, to pant and gasp through a nagging stitch:
I am not your child. But I am your child.

Hippy crack

It's six fifteen: a phosphate sky, peripheral finch. I'm
running, kicking a litter of lead balloons from verge
to kerb; their meloid bodies bounce and dent. I crush
the spent and sulky gleam of them. I'm running; this
tinny windfall chases me from Rosehill up to Belmont.
Very Hungry Caterpillars, open mouthed and out for
blood. The council makes another unsuccessful sweep.
They're fast as rats, a nuisance pewter, breeding in
bus shelters, the cul-de-sacs and car parks. Here they
are, rolling round the chicken shop. There is a girl
who says *it isn't hurting anyone*; who says they swim
like minnows, pose as hoard or shoal, depending. *Fun*
is a blimpy thing round here. A night out is a lights out,
is a nose-dived dancing Zeppelin; a bomb you can squash
like soap in your fist. It's six fifteen, the stale air quite
huffed up, and London twists in its fidgets: modems,
programs, modern toss. The working week, the slump
and puzzle of it. Mouths go anxious after bread, open
and close on the sound of aphid zeros, mating.
The tyrant swallows his tonic. And there is a girl pops
an eye at the ceiling.

Sisters under the sun

For Sogul Sur

We are *exceptional.* Our worthy endeavour, our dark idea.
Miscreant quickenings, unmade beds. A poem is pouring
our torment into the world like petrol through a letterbox.
A poem is parting our lips. Our lips part. No sound comes
out. I cannot sleep. The pillow is not safe. The pillow is
a makeshift silencer. I say my distortion into the small
of the night, the cold place at the base of the spine. I do
not dream and, no, they told me, I am *not* a poet. *Lackeen,*
the primitive spring in my blood, gaudy and poisonous.
Only the mean girls came to my coronation. I was crowned
with a decadent head wound. They tore the pages from my
books. My books had caught the war like a sneeze, trapped
between tissues. *The war? What war?* They said. Forgive
me, please. I meant *my* war, but tried to imply a definitive
sickness. I wear *my* war like a dunce's cap and stand in
the corner. *My* war is unremarkable martyrdom, white
bread, keying the side of a Ford Cortina, and *Mícheál is
dead.* My war is not their war, is not your war, is nobody's
war. A fat man in an English pub is sporting *his* war
like a laudable bruise. I wonder, do you hate him even
half as much I do? We are *exceptional,* rare birds prized for
the quality and texture of our silence. Rare birds, grooming
our plumage for pillows. The pillow is not safe. The pillow
shelters the sweet dreams of homicidal maniacs. Men,
I mean. We're inside their erring lust like figures in
a snowglobe. *Oh god, oh no.* We're running out of air.
Send help. The ice melts, and the levels rise. Drowning
now. They want to doctor your laurels like botanists. Cut
you away from yourself at the stem. They'll tie you with
twine. A greenhouse is a shallow grave, a mirror your
only source of light. *Exotic,* a serrated word they use
to sever tendons. I wonder, do you hate them half as
much as I do? I do. I do. I asked my mother *Why was I
born a girl?* She said *God cannot love
everyone equal.* Our gods are evil. Our gods
squat on personal rain clouds filing their
teeth. They ask us about our gods. They want to
photograph our cheekbones, they practice our
accents into their voicemail. We are imperfectly

adored. Desire should make us mighty, but desire
carves thin wafers of flesh from my chest. Desire
is a fist forcing its thoughtless proficiency into
the tight wet spaces inside. The birdhouse inside,
where the war lives. Our coat collars turn themselves
up on purpose. The pillow is not safe. The pillow
spreads our sleep about like an ugly rumour. Oh,
to be free of this skin. We should bask
in our *masculine egos* like sharks.

My dear Maurice

'Oh — Vivienne! Was there ever such a torture since life began! — to bear her on one's shoulders, biting, wriggling, raving, scratching, unwholesome, powdered, insane, yet sane to the point of insanity, reading his letters, thrusting herself on us, coming in wavering trembling ... This bag of ferrets is what Tom wears round his neck' — Virginia Woolf

'It was only when I saw Vivie in the asylum for the last time I realised I had done something very wrong... She was as sane as I was.' — Maurice Haigh-Wood

The body is a stranger to *deceit*; *betrayal's* another matter,
brother mine. April yet again; a season of caprice and pale
Jacquard is soon to be upon us. I shall not stir. I will remain
immaculate – one must. Mother said that beauty is a white,
unyielding power that stiffens girls like frost. I've been here
so long, and when I came I froze when spoken to, a spider
stunned by torchlight. Now, I think of you, at eight years old,
a cruelly scrutinising god, you burnt the slow blue beetle up;
you cooked him in the shipwreck of his limbs. Oh, brother
dear, I should have held this memory close and known you
better then. Do you believe that unluck gathers unluck to
itself? I do. The dirty snowball that results is *family*, or *love*.
Here I am, you tell me that I belong. Is this your love, to have
me sit and watch the earth turn among the variously wounded,
women whose sickness is militancy, who swing their arms
like soldiers, whose *lunacy* is a uniform? Is this your love?
I have no anger in me, merely ask. I'm calm. I wait for hours
before the tallest window; I do not blink, my face a witlessly
classical mask. Our Mother would approve. I seem to dream,
suspended in decorous torpor; casting these unvaried
shadows on the orange carpet. I *seem* to dream, amassing
my inertias like a sundial; lichens climb my embonpoint.
My apathy is eveningwear. And yet – the mind remains,
obstreperous and pure, a child's fist curled tight inside.
It knows this is not love, that from love's honeyed climate
I am kept, and barred, for good. Tom will not come; this
certain arithmetic splinters the hand. Tom will not come.
The girl who combs my hair, insipid with compassion, smiles
and smiles. Tom will not come. The doctors bring the heaped
precocious scorn of clever little boys. Tom will not come.
I cannot breathe sometimes; I find myself in such a rage
I tear the covers from my books; I rip their white meat with
my teeth. Sometimes. Today I am not angry, brother mine.
In some future time they'll say my body had betrayed me.
In some future time. Close up your mouth, your eyes, reseal
my letters, keep your conscience for posterity. I think I had
such life in me. I don't remember well; sometimes I see a river,
blue and gold, the bright and tattered fabric I am remnant of.

Sister Cathy

To think, I'd asked forgiveness of the wrong ghost, all my life.
We thought so much of ourselves, in our officious necromancy.
I'm being hard, I know, but someone has to be. Death's a star
that keeps on rising, no one will be honest now. Insufferable
optimist, although I swear I meant it kindly. It's not a blind
obedience I loved, I loved surrender's agate possibility. What
did I think they'd teach me? Girls have always known a world
that's bigger than themselves. I thought we would bestride
a raging sea like pirates; explode the feather pillows of a stifled
grace, and set our better angels free. To think, I'd asked
forgiveness of the wrong ghost, all my life. Ours was a venturing
faith, we said, born of the enclave, acoustic guitar, a pressing
sense of *subito!* To step out into the chaperoned-real, and hold
yourself up to the light, just once. Ours, an endeavouring
faith, to busy ourselves with youth's lithe heart; to measure
its endemic love, and tend to it like nettles. Oh, to think
of everything that might be plucked and scorned. To think
of hope's discreet extinctions, softly-softly, daily. And I had
asked forgiveness of the wrong ghost, all my life. Ivory
Madonna, whose frail severity holds no natural mother's
warmth. And Christ, on gas-mark seven, bluest flame,
a terrible burn, a solipsistic only-child. It's not a blind
obedience I loved, it's holding every doubt in turn up to
an inward jewellers' loupe; it's faith in faceted beholding,
how every day I'd stand amazed at some bright trapdoor in
myself. Or in the girls. The girls. And all the while
they learned how to walk lightly; some truths would never
take their weight. Oh, most furtive creed. When did I know?
On what occasion of the eye, of sharpest green forswearing
sky? And should I speak? And how to say? I did not do
enough. Until one day —— the early spring has bunched
my upstart mouth with flowers. I entertain the ardent shoots;
the bowl I have become inviting rain.

Francis

And this above all: that he might venture the frozen
stone at the centre of me. Nights I redouble my Antic.
Susceptible flesh. An old colonial soak, feeding his
wrist though a mackintosh sleeve the wrong way round.
I am uncoupled, both sly and wrong. Nights I've been
absolute, thoroughly juiceless, erecting myself
like a ship in a chateaux bottle. My cold ceremonious
meat, this body. Persuade the light to sway, a closer red.
Please stay, and tell me again: the pain I'm in direct
proportion to, how beauty is a maimed devouring,
sudden above all. This above all: his form, engaging
grievance. There's glass underfoot. He'd wash my
feet with glass. The immobilised mouth melts into
its own scream. A scream without edges, my mouth.
We might melt, into each other, the smudge on a lens,
on a lung. Worthy impermanence. Desire is my most
ruthless melancholy. Usurpers in every corner. Bodies
are vulgar, they keep their monsters well amused.
My softest parts appease his teeth. He hunts blind.
We appear before God, scoured and crouched. I love
this fear. He makes a fist of me. His thumb pushed into
a bloody egg.

Poem in which I attempt to explain my process

Poem in which I dream again the gun's stuttering
function, in which the sound of rifle fire comes back
at me like canned laughter, where love is a four letter
cautionary pain. Poem in which a sour grief grouts
the mouths of maiden aunts, who count their grim
keepsakes out like calories. Poem in which the old
cripple's Bombyx fists are burst on the low corner
of a tea table, where funerals are manners, ramekins,
napkins, and a picture of the Late Pope. Poem in
which I cannot sleep, wear faith like a verdict, blacken
the blackest Friday in recorded history. Poem in which
Belfast beams her paranoid telemetry, in which there
is no *past*, only *history*. Poem in which my suicide-
cousin gave everything away to the stupid utopian
ponzis of God and his chronically bothered Christian
Science. Poem in which the kitsch pity of ex-lovers
does my head in, in which I walk the streets, banging
my loss like a one man band. Battered boots, excessive
sobriety. Poem in which I do not need your pale
carnations, where I am *prodigious* with lilies. Fixed
grin awaiting wind change. Poem in which Saint
Michael appears in the rear-view mirror, a head-banging
klepto in biker boots, swinging a brick in his fist. *He* is
the saint I have the patience of. Poem in which *madness
makes the heart grow thunder*, in which I overuse the word
melancholy, in which I have a look that could *spoil
ointment.* Poem in which I am *schtum* as a straight razor,
in which *speak of the devil and he will appear*, in which
All Coppers Are Bastards. Poem in which yours is a *terror*
and mine is an *incident.* Long day of fire and indifferent
vendetta. Poem in which I dress for a fetish, latex plaything,
in which my mouth is a crack in a windshield, spreading
with the stinging stress of pebbles. Poem in which we
open up the boy, like a paper fortune teller. Poem in which
some detrimental shit set fire to a dog in the rural night.
Poem in which we glean reprisals from radio static. Poem
in which Nornia – carnival of Atypical Grace. Poem in
which *oh God, the ache in my arms*, the dirty flat, the flat
finesse of medication. Poem in which a down day is
dragging its clubbed foot. Poem in which a man's hands
move like a heat wave over me. Poem in which *fuck
everything*; the state, estate, the state I'm in, the stiff

bewilderings of experts. Poem in which I am incorrectly diagnosed. Poem in which *cultural sensitivity* is agreeing to ignore me. Poem in abject psychosis, colossal folly, in the flesh.

Saint Hellier

You called it the *Hotel California*. Among other things.
We waited around for hours; the pastel drawings dragged
their skewed perspective over the eye; their colours mumbled:
weak coffee and commiseration, Styrofoam and dandruff.
We fluttered round your scanty light like moths. We listened
to your fluids sigh in see-through tubes. *Crazy straws,*
you said. We were standing at your bed. We were standing
at the window, and there the view drooped too: gardens
with brow-beaten flowers, the sulky wending of a bus;
Edwardian pubs, sexless and semi-bulldozed. We stood
there for days, and in the corner shop they sell a migraine
cheap. We'd go for Lucozade, a paper, or for anything at
all, swinging our arms through seagulls, parking charges,
dogs of a baleful, polyglot pedigree. Orbital town, reeling
in a sour, polluted light. Beyond the main reception,
figures, smoking, paced out against the grey and early
day like cockle-pickers. We'd return to face the acid
dignity of nurses, Aleppo in the rubble of its raging
thirst, the listless griefs of cancer wards, a daughter's
thin scream, the doctor with his goblin word that won't
be bargained into meaning, hallways, insensible with
slamming doors, the latest celebrity non-event. You
wanted to know *the goss.* It all gets mixed up in our
heads, or yours. There was menial tea, and the vending
machines were massive and stoic and chaperone.
Patience was a bone I gnawed an end of when
the chapel closed. Caffeine, like a finger in a hinge.
Women: mothers and sisters, priggish with woe.
The stale air squeaked my vinyl boots, our scraped-
back hair. And you at the grand finale, singing sotto
voce: *you can check out any time you like, but you can
never leave.*

On incantation

An off-white hotel bedroom in the pokey heat of summer: here is our old calamitous melancholy, come to cull my love like a captured flag. I stand near-naked in the cock-a-doodle moonlight, and pant like a Pekingese dog for want of you.

This isn't *longing*. This is bleary need and *I want* like a dig in the ribs. So come then, fool, come pebble-brained and walking your old warped kilter, the coked-up cartoon rain dance of joyride, ceilidh, clubland. Come boy, whose thirst was a fortress, *fool boy* I couldn't reach; soft boy who trembled his hemlock alone. Come sick, in a rank lacquer of sweat, laid out cold on a camp bed, baste in the pale grease of a pickled trotter. *Fucked* or *clucking*,

come, in any way you please: courting your diffident misery like a grounded schoolboy, or pumpkin-grinned, as a quenched mess of soppy love, a hot rock wedged in your frontal manger, rokkering under a hyacinth sky. Come from the starry revile of a Belfast night, tread a threshed mile with the green reveal of spring on your breath; come from baleful grace, your scorched corner, raids and rummages, from forecourts and cafés, the red-roofed safe house – *safe as houses* – an everyday advent of open doors.

Come, because I cannot sleep. I fix grit-coffee, watch the news: riots, obesities, the ingrown godless poor who are always with us. Come, because I want a drink and wonder how we got here. All of us, with our pacts and our remorses; our tantrums and our art. I *keep it together*, recalibrate all of my cascade cravings, doubling down. And I want to tear out my hair at the roots. I see you, jinxed and drowned and everywhere, lost in your dumb recreational carry-on. I see you everywhere, you might as well come.

Ten days dead and you are mine alone, don't you know that? Ireland has her martyrs, generals, gone prophets; has fools enough in giddy, workshy plenitude. Boy, whose thirst was a hair shirt, who could not cling or scratch at *peace*, and is not needed. You belong to me, just me, just come, with olive branches, smoking roses; pale hands built for trade or menace. Come spitting, and drilled to your diamond insides. Come. The skimping, sooted, sotted North wants washing too. She can't clean up come clean without you.

The pokey heat of summer, and all day long I looked for God, but God was stubbornly curbing his alchemies. There was only the ordinary: all that sorry shit we muse and strive on. I walked all day. I thought the city would give you up, but no. The city is chemical torment and blatant absurdity; the same arrogant scrabble as always. The city is girding her loins in siege mentality, fracas, spate, and Catholic frenzy. You did not return.

I've prayed, you know, have given out with: *oh, you placid canon
saints, what can you tell me of pain?* I have prayed, gone over
and over the pallid ablutions of my faith. I have whinnied to you,
flashy and bloodsome boy, to the fucking I loved like an arcade game –
such lights and sighs. It does no good. You are not summoned
and nothing has changed. I jaywalk my penance of pacing, gesture
at traffic, bawl and scorn.

An off-white hotel bedroom, where I turn the TV on. There are
rumours, as usual, there are starlings and tirades; there is light on
the backs of my hands, public transport, strikes, insomnia. There
is hectoring and skirmish, an implausible poem or two.

Come home, before the trump tornado of my loss has done me in,
has sent me wailing, pin-wheeling. Come, or I will have to agree
with these pills that you are gone, will gild your ghost in empty
rooms no more. This, I will not accept, I cannot say. We were
magicians once. I grind my teeth, and chalk the floor. I'm wearing
red, and green. I will leave the window open, *mulo.* I will preen
my oily grief like feathers.

Citizen Pit Bull

Hey, your dog is a barking farce, is a prevalent threat to the face!
Man's best friend is a serious injury, seventy stitches, the fingers
you find in a wheelie bin! Enter Citizen Pit Bull with amber eyes.
Nobody loves him. Here he comes, my Citizen Pit Bull, attacking
the slow handclaps of Liberal Democrats; ripping the throat from
a Hunt Ball. Bitten by Brummie aggression again. An ill wind,
the Saturday pamphlet, Radio Four. Exit, pursued by pitchforks.
Citizen Pit Bull, upside-down and wagging his tail in a burning
windmill. He is mine, *magnetic north,* a love that pulls at my cells
like the sun. Uproar, storm in the shape of oblong backs, of dogs,
black waves and yellow. Dorsal curve of his clipped ears. *Hey,*
you can't handle that dog, little girl, little woman, how much
do you want for that dog? The grim event unfolds. A whining
menace, whipped to life. Here is a place where nothing is safe.
We're burning his papers like Cold War spies.

Jonah

I knew him first as *callow youth*, slender
as hydroponic skunk, his mouth a spectacle
of inkjet orchidity. He said I kissed as if
I was licking an envelope. I was fourteen,
hungry as a half-filled cistern. I wanted
to break free.

I sought him out. I sought him out behind
the pool hall, near the nettles, in the night.
I had him in a caravan, in an Airfixed frenzy
of little joinings up. I treasured his hangdog
horniness, his tangy breath, his plastery hands.

I knew him again in summer, strung out
in a regular tedium of delinquency. I was
eighteen, home for the horse fair, he
had never left, lost in the dumb mañana
of youth unemployment. I was spit-shined,
undergrad.

He sought me out. He sought me out
among my books and bed sheets, clamant
masturbator who always called at the wrong
moment; groaning, gaunt and grainy
as footage of Roswell, peevish and smutty
and smelling of hash, of wet cement.

I saw him last in the dank grotto
of his Blackrock squat, bent low
like blowing glass; one of seven
skellybone boys in dirt and shreds
of denim, delicate and fidgeting.
He hit me up for a tenner.

I sought him out. I seek him out, even
now, his mohawk crushed like a sucked
brush, his mouth twitching with baccy
and tattle.

Because we were kids under the same
begrudging blue; the same squat roofs,
flat and terse. I seek him out on the rec
ground. I seek him out when I am *home*,
catching my breath in Milltown among
the cold reproach of the stones.

Sailing from Jökulmær

This I have brought back to you: a granulated light against our puritan and thoroughgoing dark, that night our channels narrowed, and in remembrance we traced those storm-taut gauntlets to the open sea. We thought of you; our small boat reeled and tipsied like a spark, and we were mute and queasy with the cold. These memories are not enough, and so I brought you gruff ancestors, wrapped like baby teeth in paper napkins, packed between the flannelettes in thermal snug. I gathered all the arrowheads, all trinkets, charms and thunderstones. I learnt to sing your songs: your cold morose bewitchments found half-hidden in the hills. Snow-glutted farms, the faults and springs, the sting and taste of failure; ice and basalt, blighted crop. *This* I have brought back to you: grim thimble of black sand, a photograph: these people were your people, lean and fearful pilgrims; upright dynasties that split their bows on slick green rock. These people were your people, these faithful and unmerry ghosts, unravelled with all hands. I offered you their wassail and their isinglass; their offal and their crochet lace. Their god, a cramped mistaking sworn to in the dark. You did not see yourself in them. I handed you their church instead, an off-white spire, a pallid tusk. I showed you stained glass, paschal musk. I had smuggled their Christ through customs as a splinter under my nail. Old woman, I had conjured up the dehydrated daylight, stink of fish, a map marked *Thule*, the way a whale might be a monster, sleek disturbance in the eye. I told you of my husband's hands, the headland's feral gloom, and morning's caustic coffee taste, the sulphur in the water. It was not enough for you. The doped pearlescence of the sea, my heart in all its slippery malfunctioning; impression cast in plaster of his every skittish kiss. You are unmoved. I fashioned you an amulet from Jólakötturinn's teeth, and scooped the stars like mushrooms in my skirt. I gave you all my sad wayfarer's wealth: how gannets make their frothy wounds in waves, slipping like pearl-handled knives between the shoulder blades. Old woman you belonged here, you should wear a bib of foam while drinking pints of mead from steins I chisel out of bone. But you would not remember, corpsey green and violet lights astray, askew, and wandering. The thin black ice, salt cod with every single thing. You have no need for stories now, explore instead your own embattled, stark frontier. If I should tell you where I've been you would not care, you do not hear. Out there beyond the car park, London harps her asphalt theme. You're livid with the nurses; your words rise up like mountains, sharp as little fishing hooks. You spit words like a sailor still. These fragments of perfected spleen.

Matthew in Heaven

I see him still: a cat creates itself anew from oblong
shadows under cars. He grins and takes possession
of a bad idea. A girl applies her leeches to his skin,
a glossy pout that sucks the blood. Another time, he
stands in a furious quantity of rainbow light. He is
prince of the rampant solar. His blood, a delicate
viral cipher. Nineties rave, discrepant slang, a kiss
that comes like a twisted ankle. The summer heat
pressure-cooks his silhouette. Another time, witchy
and thin, he is sequinned and tainting the snakebite
with gossip. His long white opera gloves are waving,
wavering, silky seabed parasites. Another time, his
empty flat creaks like a ghost train; a spider unpicks
her circle, retreats into his teaseled wig. He thumbs
his own eyes shut and turns, to a seraph on a velvet
stool: *Corrupt me like a Borgia Pope* he slurs into
an ice and never-ending. I dream him still:
the victims arrive for the fancy dress ball in
their monster makeup and three-tiered gowns. His
wound is a diamond rejoinder, set in a difficult
face. The chandelier above him exaggerates
a masterpiece: Titian chorus dancing round
their severed heads like handbags. *Brother where
art thou?* there's something crawling in the water,
our perishable chemistry. A fist will eclipse
a crooked tooth, the window brittle into
butterflies. Men will thunder down South
London streets like centaurs in Ben Sherman
shirts. It's in the dogshit breath of letter boxes,
the slant graffiti sloping up a stairwell, a roman
salute descending from a Sunday sky. *We* are
hoisting our fear like a pirate flag. *He* fixes
an amateur daiquirí: *Fuck you with a fist full
of false red nails.* I see him still, he's dancing
on, on broken heels.

The accidental death of a plagiarist

I think you want me to suffer;
sit in, night after night, swigging
the caustic miso of my own
repentant tears; surviving on scraps
and surpassingly snubbed, I become
meagre and suave, in love
with my own vaulting contrition.

You honestly want I should suffer,
days like these, rehearsing
the folklore of my downfall. Ouch!
Subsisting on the charity of dolts,
jostled by the lukewarm cruelty
of Guardian readers, assistant eds.
It stings, like a tweaked nose.

I do suffer, risking the strip-
lit standstill of Tesco, at night. Panic
buying in my jimjams, and a tight
glut of words, pushing at my guts.
I was a poet, but now I mooch
by the cans of cranberry jelly; muster
my haggard bravado for a pity-fuck
amongst the frozen peas. It really does
come down to this, has come to this.

I suffer, I tell you. My loss
throbs, I am depressed. I drink
like hardboiled film noir.
My Mum is very cross.

And I deserve better, yes,
I've suffered for your art.
Exemplary penitent, gorgeous
boy. I told you I was sorry.

What more do you want? Should I
slash something to prove it? Should I cry
Wolf! Wolf! Wolf! or *The sky is falling down!*
Oh, please forgive me, I shall wither and die.

Yeah, this has been a very difficult time
for me. I look forward to regaining your trust.

Remedial dog

After Roddy Lumsden

Pierrot, fanged * feral eunuch * punch drunkard * pauper
lunatic * lunatic * Cowardly Lion, whimpering into his
mane * two-man tent put up askew * pantomime horse *
short bus * unmade bed * silo * fallen rocket stage * tundra *
two-seater sofa * Boris Karloff, lit by burning torches *
genetic misdemeanour * Prince Myshkin with a flick
knife at a school disco * fourth stooge * Bash Street
Kid, embarrassed at his Bar Mitzvah * Ronnie Kray
sucking a paintbrush in Broadmoor * folklore * bogey *
boyband blonde caught out by a tabloid * whiskey priest *
acid casualty * Howard Marks * Hunter S. * Bez, for fuck's
sake * prison bimbo * developmentally moot * numb *
urchin * goof and balk * banter with an ambulance * fifties
ditz * pneumatic mouth * snap and flinch * Baby Jane,
throwing a hissy * Cuchulain fighting the sea * I've written
a letter to daddy * psycho killer, qu'est-ce que c'est?

A backward dark

I grew like a twisted tooth, and every day was a backward dark, and delving awkward into morning, met by soft syndromal light let into rooms through cracks in glass and gaps in brick. How should I spend my *precious* time? These hours of stricken and hiccuping mien, and *what did you think would happen?* Left alone to my own gaunt indifference, with nothing to get up for. They said they could not help me, professional obsessives in glum and underfunded rooms I crawled to and then back, by ugly alleyways and flats, breathing in an air of eager menace; psychotic riposte, urine and homicidal shoplift. Inside, a dead, dry plant with crispy bacon leaves, expired medication. They said they could not help me. I am less than nothing, an excrescence in the eye of an overworked GP. What should I do? Slump my misshapen shoulders at the desk, survive on sheepish chivalries, the profligate affinities of friends who say they *love* me and then don't call for days? Or drag my debt to be the subject of slack whispers in the local bar, to hide from crowds of people with my old cowering proficiency. An online forum told me *you are not your worst day*, but this disease puts out more roots than branches, and anyway, there's nowhere left to go but down. They said they could not help me. Grey-brown fish food flakes of snow. My mirror is a study in malnourishment. I drop my untidy shadow by the bed like crumpled clothes. I *try* to work, at anything at all. I do not want to live like this, prostrate before the bailiffs yet again. I do not want to live. A book is better eaten than drowned. Evicted, unemployable, people like me *shouldn't aim too high*. It's Friday and the blackly estimated self is slipping. I wish this pain electric, to exit via the fingertips in sparks. But it does not, it is a dull and stumbling blow, the cold slap of another wave. This pain makes nothing. It's all I'm good for, born for, groomed to droop, to wheedle in a stuttering rank to clinics and to agencies, and *what is wrong with you?* Burning up with shame, its red-faced sensibility. In university I learnt to tell *suffering* from *punishment,* and much good has this done me. I grew like a twisted tooth, with dirt at the crown and rot at the root.

'What it is'

It's like how the blank page thinks it's better than you and you go to risky basements dressed up all exhaustive and feline and listen to glitchy techno, its ringtone pneumatics drilling the front of your skull like baroque and switchy birdsong, and you're better off, you know, you're better off out of the suffering mesh, a muzzy shambles with feelings a forgivable squall like rain on a long weekend. I'm not good at texting I'm not good at drinking until saying your name is an allegation and it's four a.m. in the lurking jellied light chilling out among the hardboiled poor and halves of limes and the bar has the curvy incognito of a CAT scan I think and the speakers trickle glad tidings past my pewter lobes. I put poems in my phone I couldn't find a pen but look now the screen's no bigger than an After Eight mint I think it is a very specialist form of derision this pretending you can hear me. It's blurring I'm blurring the cultivated prism of a fly's eye, the folksy stifle of smothered in kisses, how I hate a song about white British girls falling in love how I hate it to my skittering, niggling proteins and what're youse looking at? How her iPad is a violent digest and she's like a hen-party full of strident consolations don't cry, pet but I'm not crying. I'm not good at texting at drinking I prove goofy in the too-cool downstairs, size-plus tomboys making eyes at me 'cause I have a smile as nervous as knee-jerk as automatic doors and the butch ones like it and you're better off, you know, better off not needing a number a name their dross doesn't get in your eyes, doesn't get in your Ph.D proposals and propped-up bed-head like it gets into mine 'til the permissive fizz of their white wine is a shuddering pulse in the sinuses. I've got a name and I'm not all right: these oranges these lemons these drums and basics, the components of my trepidation and I want coffee thick as topsoil no I want gin with lip-smack lemon no I want grimy kalimotxo I want I want doesn't get. I'm saying your name till it beheads itself tripping the tongue like a fugitive limerick and I am not awake not really not awake enough for chatups fucking obvious as a fire-extinguisher and no I know he doesn't love me and not awake enough for the shameless hardcore canopy of London stars, puking on the pavement, mis-mated and ladders in my tights. I'm not good at going on my knees and having you barter your echo near the nape of my neck where my name is your name close to the chip-fat scourge on my spine. It's like go away spazzing gravity and stumbling under busses and the cool verge of the bowl in the jacks like an inverted Saint Paul's and I want to shut all my doors forever and not be saddled with your bragging ghost. I'm no good at sending texts drinking smothered in kisses in party-frocks in silk-gloved swag like First Communion. You are a dead battery, M. This is what it's like. For the Bereaved (proper noun). For the living. Blah-blah forever. I hate men…

The difference between

i.m. M.J.H.

This is not London: these cold, encumbered houses
where First Light is polar and philistine. Youse told me
that, that every city's Sunday is *broken open diff'rent*.
Belfast, then, in her minutely scrutinised wakening,
lifts up her trees like trophies. It is Ulster turning her talk-
to-the-hand to the hills. I don't want to dream this dream.
My body aches.

I won't sleep in. I will not sleep. I will not sleep my walking,
walk my sleeping. I will be awake and say at last, out loud
my grief is not a dream.

Yes, this is really happening. I mope my morning cup,
wallow in music: the mad glitching skirl of our breadline
braggadocio; feral euphorias, fanfare of aggro. I dance.
I mime my dancing, wringing the wanderlust out of
my hands. I imagine you into a song that sounds like fog
lifting, knowing full well you'd have been unimpressed,
said *juss like a Tenement Westie to temper disaster with
singing!* And I'm singing.

But oh, there are jigs, love, and then there are reels.
And somewhere between the thumped gut of the bodhrán,
the twitterpated squeak of the fiddle; the grim correctional
whine of the flute, we came undone. We *all* came undone,
not just you, badluck bedouin, drowned on the wide, unruly
margins of the sea.

You said *faith is a cracked skull and a cup of mud.*
You said *fuck 'em all*, them and their milestone
martyrdoms, doomed youth and retinue heroics.
Fuck 'em all, you said, you meant The Land
and her agonies of erosion; the polymorphous
North, a perverse instrumental of pipes and wire.

We lived for a while. We tried. You tried, but you
cried in the night, your long feet itched for the Lower
Falls, a boyhood bedecking itself in stones. Hungry
as only half-breeds can be, we grabbed for each other
those days when remorse was neither worn or swallowed.

And we lived for a while, got free for a while, of bigots
drilling fingers into stingy fists, of a God only God enough
to daub or bray; of sink estates, their malice either pandered
to or fattened. I had you for the best of the worst of the years.

But yes, this is really happening. This morning is yours.
The North you could not claim claims you. I will go down
to the shore and give you back: a spree of grey salt water
sky descends to meet the day this crescent moon in feckless
penitential vanishing. I cannot be wise inside my wanting
you. I want to call out *stay* –

I don't mean *stay*, I mean *go*, tangent and fleeting,
in rain, on air, a vapour of meth and petrol. I mean
to say that some days freedom is attrition, and those
days the living are awkward and spare.

Go, then. And I will walk away. I will pass the ruin
of the prison, sleeping like a sphinx. I will live. I will
live and learn the difference

between what's lost and what is missing;
between what's tied, and what is bound.

Centennial

i

Saturday's mongrel amusements collapse under
their own soft weight, and we're waiting. Fenian
earworm by half past ten; the *Yanks* with their
accents at half-mast, buying up the earnest merch
of Easter. Our omnivorous lens eats everything:
sunlight, a tinted photogasm spread across your
shoulders. On giant screens the dead exaggerate
their vanishing, and history is made of what?
Infinity of barricades, gaunt chastity of wives;
a child whose smile has all the feudal swiftness
of an axe falling. We blink the spring and are
wanly succoured. All of us shiver, and catch on
the cold air like kites.

ii

Low houses, intemperate with flags, and pubs
are ugly with the shame they are put to. Stoney's
quicklime sky, still wearing whiteness as
a reprimand. This is *no country*. Old men, in their
skirmishing frailty, tapping the uneven streets
with aluminium sticks. We walk to the museum.
These are faith's inglorious tokens, or time's: one
pair of cracked glasses, a censored letter, scapular,
the gap-toothed smile of a broken comb. Women
leave so little behind, limbs and sighs all rinsed
or folded in dust. *This is us*, you say. We are
testing our pedigree, against English, against
death's sucking function. Lilies congregate
on every bend in the road like spies; a rainbow
overflows its cistern, we are showered in
a counterfeit gold.

iii

There's a fine line between *exile* and *cunning*.
Sudden shower, the smell of wet wool, teenage
boys carousing on a roundabout. Girl whose face
is bland grief and Airwalk trainers, slumped on

her last sulking nerve before the kiosk. Amateur
family, the kids in green ribbons. A beige dog
elongated by suffering. I am running now. I'm
through the park, along the quay, and running,
from forebears who have buried their dead at
midnight's creaking yard arm, or served a penal
six-month for the grubby sod they sucked
the roots of. I'm running from women, unavailable
to grace, handled like a horse fair, an umbrage
of gums and inspected flesh, of nightwork up in
Monto. Bent for breath, I dip my head to what
the moist earth whispers: *we are what we are,*
girl, we are what we are.

iv

Coastal road, fatigued with flowers. A small
town of near-sighted affections is wearing
spring like a hair shirt. Woman in the café,
her smile is a Twilight Zone; her hands
wrestle her gestures, stunt kites swooned in
the bruising air. We follow the peninsula:
wooden bridge, then Mary, our Virgin of the
Windswept Vertigoes, beaming her bright
ideas at the ships. There are waves, detritus,
jeeps and gulls; exhaust, corrosion, panting
dogs. There are small gods, adjusting their
crosses like radio antennae. *Listen.* I listen
for the sound of his voice. I listen until my
frequencies skip. He is the muddy faith this
home has made a compass and a suction of.
Flowers unfold like paper fortunes,
drooping mottos meaning *peace.* I
have held a hot coal in my mouth so
long, a pain that is more than this
dutiful sorrow. My song should be
an anthem of hands. *Mise Éire,*
pronounced error.

Visiting Prometheus

I get lost coming up, standing around at a discoloured junction, waiting for
the lights to change. Shop fronts bristle with discounts; the afternoon sun is
a dazzle on handlebars, natty dreads, and indiscriminate piercings. It's hot,
hot enough for bursting bin bags; hot enough for cancer, sleeting into cells.
Which way to go? I ask the girls with salted earth complexions, the drizzle-
witted men outside of Wetherspoons, and finally a boy, all bantam swagger
and slouchy lust. I remind him of *his mother!* so he walks me to the corner,
and from there I get the bus. I am afraid. I know too well what to expect.
Your forecast is a frozen hell we'll skate upon like children. There are such
fears as no one dares to name. The hospital is looming like the punch-line to
some racist joke. You know, I've tried to be *resigned*. There isn't any *sense*
to make, and nobody is *saved*. I know this too, and I listen to you repeat my
name, a silted, flattish sound that no face fits. You've moved beyond the laws
of recall now. I force myself to stay, but cannot hold your hand. Your skin
is dry enough to strike a match, and if I touched I'd run the risk of raising fire.
I hate you then, the way your blood became accustomed to its poisons; your
flightless spiral down into depression's praline velvet dark. Why should *you*
escape alone? You were as alive as me, swinging your arms through a starless
park, your hood collecting coloured leaves. Somebody said you *lived without
fear.* But all your eerie pleasures curdled into vertigo, and *here* are no more
chances to be reckless or be brave. I get lost coming back. Your doctors are
true poets, finesse their fine distinctions: *strength* is not the same as *health*, so
don't be fooled. I won't. I seem to make you worse. I sit beside you for a while;
misread the way the light behaves. An aluminium-coloured sky, a storm you
turn towards without expectancy or dread. *You* are free, are dispossessed of all
the yawning pains we call *remorse*. I'll tell you what contrition is, it's boredom
with our past mistakes. Disgust breeds in the meat of this idea. You said that
you were *sorry* once. Who were you *sorry* for? I want to hit you. My fist cannot
discharge its harm, it waits, and while it waits the ugly, flashy family griefs are
gathering like groupies. I'll lie, I'll say *it's fine*, and feed you fruit so soft it comes
apart in your mouth like a child's sigh. I've been so lost. They tell me I am
good. I'm not. Your veins are like the casts of worms in wet sand; you look
so small. And on the coppery margins of your blood the medicine floats
like a shallow canoe. Don't rock the boat. Pretend that stillness might preserve
you. I'll relate the day's indifferent events, trying to talk you back into
yourself. It will not work. I'm angry, and somebody says: *Hey, men drink,
it's what they do.* You sleep and so I take the bus back through the skunky
puzzle of the lanes. I wish that it was winter, when you and I once climbed
a hill, that time when we were clean and free, and tipped our heads right
back to catch at midnight's loose atomic feathering of snow.

The seven habits of highly affective people

You know, I *am* a little bit backward. Spent half a life in putting swine
before a trough of pearls. That sort of thing. There is a faith not *kept*, but
made. And work, the self-inflicted ethic no one holds me to. I take my
misfit consolations in alone. As in insomnia's scuttling malady. Poetry
helps less than coffee, truth be known. There's pleasure in refusing
things: the crummy lusts of undergrads, a bowl of indiscriminate meat,
your *kind regards*, my own debilitated wit at six a.m. when I believe I'm
somebody. I'm not. Most times that's clear, and I can see myself for my
remedial breed; I can see myself, recalcitrant and aspy, and striking
a match on my noseblown sleeve. Mornings, better shunned than met,
when curtains cling together in conjunctive light, when someone said
we're made from all the shit that we forget, the self that squeaky polo's
hole you poke a little finger through. But *I* live by the eye, by grim
eidetic frenzy. There's nothing I've forgotten yet. It is uneasy, the onion
chopping work of writing down, and when I pirate Michael's light to
mixtape melancholia, oh, I loathe the aching face of me. But there are
other days, less stumblebrained, when bed-settees will shrug me up,
and life will find me primed for polyphonic outburst, or the slant delights
of London. Brick Lane days, and Brixton, how I love her cagey chutzpah!
And *psycho-ceilidh, qu'est-ce que c'est*, in some dim bar where they are
slicing hemispheres of lime, and *whoa there!* I will blow you off your feet
with mania's breakneck gale-force. Nights I'm so *Sharknado*, in a skirt
and steel toe boots. It's true, I'm not so hot at *in between*, oscilloscopic
skittishness my stock in trade. You know, I *am* a little bit backward.
The brain's dyslexic lurgy on a low day, pulling my arms around myself
as if resisting crucifixion. Or geeky, out of doors, trying to read in boozily
skirmishing parks, homesick, fraggle on caffeine, and singing *let us howl*.
Those days I have the tryptamine affinities I build with bus stop *loonies*,
acid mascots, disappointed ponytails; a tribe of brush-sucking obsessives
spoiling for dystopia on locked wards in plastic sandals. I've got a roll
of honour: *Henry Darger, Mary Barnes…* I'm not alone. There is a faith
where Mary flaunts her opalescent pedigree, with Rita and Lucia,
shimmying to session music; big haired backing band in sequined doo-wop.
Yes, I know, but I have always been the snaggletooth technician of my own
bolshie fate, and *crazy is as crazy does* in Catholic school, with perishable
spellings making chaos out of crayons. What gets you through is knowing
things, a disillusioned acumen, the taigy slang you run your mouth
with afternoons, or scooting full of threadworm in assembly. Do you
understand? There's method. I am still me, despite incurable karma,
and biting the hand that feeds, a spooked horse shying at sugar.
I am still me, despite the stale fertility of sink estates, and every cheque
I failed to cash. I *am* a little bit backward. You'll find me tilting my
broomstick at puritans; you'll see me coaxing water, uphill to a nag.

Special needs

And who said of the heart, *the heart has its own jaundiced folklore?* Wasn't me,
standing there with a basket of Valentines, defrosting a red mess on the lino floor.
I have this kind of fuckwit fluency with love; I'm more articulate than capable.
I told you once *I like to sit where I can see the exit*, and you took it as a metaphor,
which proves you didn't know me then – or ever. Does it matter? We don't *do*
dinner, the extrovert tableau of couples, in restaurants arranged like cots in army
hospitals, these neat white squares with napkins folded into nurses' caps. Well, fuck
that noise. Your nights are gorged on gulyás and pampushki; black bread in low
light on a low sofa, low fire on a low-moaning flame. This is home, the peasant
compulsion I rattle my pans with, the weight in the belly by which I bind you,
again and again, and who said *love has cast out fear?* The heart in its botched nose-
job aesthetics, a reddish pulp we rub salt into. I am still afraid. Long days, fumbling
but sturdy; down but not entirely out. Sometimes the soul flickers – and when I say
soul, I picture something like the steam off my tea – sometimes the *soul* flickers,
darts and struts its absentminded shadowplay. Those days I feel myself to be alive.
We pick out veg. I bake the bread. We keep my *levels* up. Young Frankenstein, my
chemistry is guesswork. That's okay. A record on, with vintage Nick to nurse
my *abby normal* brain. Who said the heart had anything to do with it? A Bombay
Sapphire sort of moon, the inundated eye is sifting sparks. I go down like a lead
balloon. Your bossy kiss. Our pit bull barks.

The very last poem in the Book of Last Things

The plug in the neighbour's kitchen makes a little living click / like a cricket / anthems to insect separatism / Muldoon's rank gnashers / a regular Mr Ed / Michelin-starred tosspot / canonised decrepitude / a photo-negative Agincourt, his fingers raised in silhouette / I will be here / I am always here / my sneering ennui / practiced villain in a white van veering / verily, this is my town / herringbone boys in porkpie hats / how *nothin' ever change, oh no* / girls in frostbite bevies, bleak midwinter / kick up your heels / ashveloped in cigarette shelter / codename cloudy, cross yourself / the creaturely solving of bodies / meat-packing laggards with mean, clear smiles / factory lasses en masse / their visitant tradition / mouths propped open like doors left ajar / the horse has bolted / were you born in a barn? / the bible is a catalogue of baby names / girls, their considerate grip on your fancies / her head is a tawny bulge / I am here / I will always be here / insufferable fauna / lily-titted girls / the crude physics of a vigil / a surf of shattered sound / this is my town / the disciplined triage of yearning / tilt on my pivot against the custom's post / *Michael*, she says, dropping her blastoff flatteries like small change / *Michael, Michael* / describing a delicate tightening gyre / her eye, a timid pinwheel / boyfriends pink to their pauper-core, the worse for drink / flagrant parade / pasture of flags / faces become brute totems / an imposing Porsche / a nonchalant dog / the property of civic leaders / their pert wives combination-locked with gin / swampy lips in glasshouse affluenza / dogwood coral hectic red / dowry of stars / an ovulate moon / and now the militant cripple's syringe / an oversexed surprise / his popcorn kernel mitts, puffed like thought balloons / I am here / I am here too / and the turbulent priest with his guts hanging out and no one knowing what to say / wincing and riveted small-town boys whose north was a fertile phoneme / popped like a lightbulb / an overlit egg / Muldoon with his insider's small-fry / flats, in their satellite diocese beaming becalmed on reruns of Dallas / oh, in the drizzled tizzy of the rain, her hair all hanging in gym-rope plaits / she crackles like a masterpiece / slack lank lather of love's young dream / the mediocre ballast of a cautionary heart / herself in all her fetching scarcities / the mothers misfiring a nightmare into Catholic guilt and tinnitus / paying a pound for an orange sky / to quiver at a migrant Mass for the sour muddle of border towns / a decked wife is a shining lamp in the rare good giddy-up of the pub / ticklish hills beneath the tension wires / dry heaving boys / in dormitory peristalsis / cry for their mammies or profess themselves amazed / I am here / tight-lipped as an oyster, shocked-mute / the town, my town, under its drenching bell / picket of limp saints, guarding the graves / Christ is a cracked gasket tonight / a remedial fuck with a wagging tongue / in blizzard telepathy, reaching out / I am Michael, Michael since sixty-nine / and the regulars / Spandau / twisting again / her slaked curves summing things up / a scribbled revision of falling boys / girls in concrete conjuration

/ jinxed cement / bleating, butterfly-stroking glass / *enough*, he says / she says enough / corporal dementia / gross ore, a cheekbone flayed of paint / mine / the doctrine of what is solid, clambering anger that pulls itself from pools / wishy-washy waterlogged and moonwalk-slow to move / spooning exquisites on trampled straw / that boy with ruby-slippers for stumps, I know / and kindness crows like a phone / faith, hope and Major fucking Barbara / replenished terror, infected pellets / spongiform forgetfulness / for children / for micro-chipped students / for the trite *inkblots of blood* / boys' blood / the peacewall warped in the rain / rapping the city a final reminder / thug knucklebone splitting a lip / I have seen it / Michael, I am Michael / four men went to mow damp daylight into cloisters / clusters / ten men on derelict requiem blasted / went to mow / stringing along on filament's thin trapeze / the wire that is the wire-walker / a solitaire tribute dumb as hunger / at three in the morning I am Michael, fishing the roving river clean / and every mill pond is a socket / customary tourniquet / her red hair / agile, ex-lover / I cannot unsee.

Us too

For Exmouth, and its escapees

i

And at the knackered traffic lights, the *lads,* led about by their soft-boiled
bellies like pregnant seahorses; regimental maniacs in berets, khaki slacks
and symptomatic tattoos, checking their reflections in their steel toe-caps.
It's Friday night, and I am walking the tusky ramparts of our *beautiful coastal
town.* Crossing the road by the fountain, I smile at a bony-shouldered band
of amphetamine featherweights, young boys bitching their brittle Polari in
local parks where broken railings fix their bayonets. I walk, and I'm
watching the women, old women, women in acrylic skin and slit up skirts
and circus stilts, preening their screams in a nightclub queue. Their eyes
are dressed in injury, they wince and strut; the curb becomes a catwalk of
hot coals. I have seen them, squeezing defeat into too-tight shorts. Hey,
don't laugh, the world turns on its thirst, you know? The world turns, on
a thousand fetish devastations. No word is *safe.* I heard them say*: You'll be
scraping your face off the back of his hand.* I'll be scraping my face off for years. It's
Friday night, dear God, and there is a girl, young girl, sucking a hardboiled
silence, cut right down to her tight pink passing-sacred; all thin white arms
and long wet hair, who hangs around her *boyfriend's* neck like a broken
stethoscope. No, no heart to hear. That girl is me. I see myself, undoing my
smile like the top button of a shantung blouse. How I court their brawling
foreplay. Lose count of the times I heard someone say: *It'll all end in tears.* A
minor vice, a little statutory angst, summer's giddy commerce on the corner
in the evening. Or, those seasick seaside mornings, flaunting my disorder by
the boat swings, skittish in a miniskirt. A blowjob or a stick of rock; a loose
tooth and a broken nose. Pain is our roseate intercourse. There's *coercion*
God, and then there's *force.* At the traffic lights, the *lads.* Our eyes collide
like marbles. I'm leatherette and penny sweets, and *sexy.* They said I was
sexy. I feel about as *sexy* as a two-seater second-hand sofa, a busted spring
in my empty belly. So scuffed, I am, so worn. There's a girl who, night
after night, will polish her most affordable fear. That girl is me. And a *lad*
looms up once more, a video game glow round him, big as an end of level
boss, he's swinging his arms through the slutty gloaming. He grabs me by
my sleeves; he drags me past the sagging wrecks of blackened bandstands,
wind-distorted portacabins. I'm on my knees beneath the beer-gut of an old
pavilion. The reek of fish and week old fat. He leaves my mouth a smashed
mess of slang and teeth. Woke up on the wrong side of the war: *I'll school
you, you pikey caant.*

ii

Worse things happen at sea, they said, and *what did you expect?* And I'm thinking
of you now, ba-lamb, bestie, the ways in which you understood. There are days
that I contain you, my own controlled explosion. The ways we shared the dolorous
geographies of *home*; the way that *home* had made a fetish out of splendour,
benediction, reverie. There is no *safe* word. No word is safe. Bottomless duty, gilded
fate, a beauty we were born imploring. How we adored the Paschal musk and
chorus of Compline; the way the lady Saints inclined their heads, girding a
devious grace in groups like school-gate gossips, how they might blow a scented
mercy you could treasure like a kiss. We knew no better then. There was nothing
better for us to know. Oh, my most Catholic ghost, I still dream about your mouth,
succulent and fated and twice the size of itself against a motley, potholed sky. Your
kiss was like pink fairy lights inside of me. Loss is not the word, not *de icit*, but
wound, this pain, both abject and succinct, and no I will never drink myself free.
Four and twenty blackbirds baked inside this grief, this keening extremis. No
prestige grief we plump like pillows on a sickbed, but something with yellowy
incisors, stripping the meat from a glistered phrase. *Tell me, what did you expect? The
Lord moves in mysterious ways.* You knew how it felt and you knew what it meant, and
you spent the rest of your empty days acquainting God with the back of your
head. I remember us haunting your bedroom mirror with our failed symmetries,
hollow-eyed, companionably jaded – feral, defiled, and exiled from the neck down,
pushing our ugly consumptive luck. Oh, my bright jinx, my strictest-shining
Catholic ghost, you remembered too well too. Left me what was left of you. I'm
stood in the photonegative light of some shitty hospital corridor, wringing my
hands and rapidly blinking. The tired eye tries to free itself from the shock it
stepped in. *Dead.*

iii

I dreamt of it again, lie still until I'm sane. The dream retreats, but leaves its
curdled traces. The school is worst, where boredom makes the minutes swim,
where the low ceilings stunted our growth, where I was a child, lisping and
conspicuous to history; suggestible poppet with braided hair, the barer of a
deformed faith that clutched at beads, a face that didn't fit. Where you were a
child, prodigal of famine and infliction, bygone pogrom, occupation and eviction.
Half breed. Bad seed. Black sheep. Mad cow, bovine on dopamine, slurring her
girlhood, I could not run, could only sweat the dread of barefoot threat in dusty
halls with all the windows painted shut, a stale and violent light outside. Inside the
proper girls, with crop-circle smiles, who sharpened their collective whisper like a
shiv and smirked my gremlin pedigree: *Gyp bitch! You botched abortion!* The boys,
aggrandised and Neanderthal, scholars of the picked scab, the sucked knuckle, the
untucked shirt. Tumescent cretins, snickering under their breath. They followed

me home. Blighted desire had tightened their guts, they took disfigured joy in causing pain. Just like their fathers, brothers, future sons: You slag! You slut! And I was cornered with exhaustion, writhing like a salted slug. Cher sings *Gypsies, tramps and thieves*. Big fucking laughs from the peanut gallery.

iv

And for the longest, dear God, I couldn't speak of this. My mouth was a glass house, gathering stones, stoned and phobic on Seroxat and Sertraline. Days spent redacting a dark eye with liquid liner, losing weight, becoming shallow as a footprint in wet sand. For the longest time I'd close my eyes and smell the sea, and brewers' yeast, and boot polish. For the longest time I'd smell the lino, chalk dust, desks: dirty grey, and barnacled with chewing gum. I'd close my eyes and feel the stingy and complicit looks of teachers boring into the back of my skull.

v

Mr B is bad breath and soiled ambition. His face swims like a boiled shirt, his skin the white of unsigned plaster casts; he has the long front teeth of a talking horse. In a rank mood he leers and reels toward me. Do you remember how we prayed back then? To God on his gilded battlements: *Sweep 'em up or strike 'em dead, dear God.* He never did. Social worker measures out her well worn spite in meticulous inches. She's a *local girl.* Her smile is frowsy industry, coastal erosion, and economic stalemate. She doesn't care that a boy has worn me like a secret on his lips; she cannot help me, can't tell me how to make a poem from a fistful of wet earth, how to dislocate my shoulders and keep on swimming. Hey, the world turns on its thirst, you know? On the scurvy lusts we must remake ourselves from daily. Two young girls, too young, tricked out in torrential dresses, smiling their slow dissolve into camera. Savants of resurrection.

X (mouth)

Being both hazard and reactance, you are electricity. Being
both pact and proof, the measure and the evidence. You are
conjurework and hoodoo, a bestowing and a banishment.
Science fiction, fascist ballot; the error and the choice. You
are rootwork, the graded curve. Robert Johnson waiting at
a crossroads for his cardinal direction. Pornography or
Christogram. You magnify, you capture, you're a sinister
fork in the cause. A blackmailer's signature. Righteousness,
crime, asymmetrical warfare. You are nexus and crisis,
the indication and the absence. Being both sanctum and any
racy fact. A forced confession with a shaky hand. You are
corrupt and you're inviolate, a friend to the oppressed.
Emblems, implications. You move through yourself
to arrive at yourself. Negate and multiply, complicate.
Dispossession. Made manifest. Made minus. Less than
yourself. Landmine, dancer's mark. Buried treasure, gallows
drop. Being a failed chromosome. Designates unwanted girl.

Fear death by water.

dead / sea

music for suicide

to arrive at the edge of the sea, uncertain as a wedding guest swaying alone at the shallow end of a depopulated dance floor. or to be standing very straight and very still, and wearing all the glamour you have borrowed from disaster: the lisping wounds of gangland, global weirding's long, black ecological cosh. *stunning.* you put their *lights out.* vamper. you are *very modern*, atonally sexy, full to the teeth of a pouting doom your lips purse into all involuntary. you want to cry: *fuck me on a pile of dirty money!* you have seen too many music videos. you are in love, with the gun's fatal tumescence, kurt cobain *painting the town* with his spag bol brains in a fever dream. *never mind.* there's a special quality to the light here, like wading waist deep in a slowly developing photograph. they couldn't begin to tell you about beauty, approaching the marbly seaside dark down the wrong end of a telescope. they couldn't begin to tell you: how beauty resides in being unformed. you always thought that loss could be lavished upon us like love. you suffered so many arrogant kisses, debunking your mouth with a mouth in the night. *intimacy* is a hand trapped between hot folds of flesh. you admit it freely, you do not know how to feel, but you are *so* lost now, like peter pan, estranged from his shadow. your dead are never coming back, and you don't want to feel. the morning's sharp insult like salt against the skin. you want an extravagant disgrace, a sorrow sleek and fierce as all hell breaking loose or what's the point? yours is not the irreproachable grief of virgins, crossing themselves at a fork in the road. your grief is the place where farce and shame will intersect in memory. ask him again: *how could you?* oh, your love has its masochisms and its vertigoes, its wounded melodrama: *how could you?* the black lagoon he's creature to disturbs the subtle function of an artery like lust. he flirts a better pain than yours, revels his infliction in a dazzlescape of lights on snow, a bed of velvet devastations. oh, a better pain than yours, a slow pain spread with ardent cunning. away in a manger, his big mid-brain is chemically coddled. candled, curdled. the ancients knew how women went deranged with grief and wandered the earth tearing their hair. the gods don't favour you, leave them to their omissions and dominions. the gods do you no favours. you have failed, you lost another, and only the sea accepts you now. you lit a fire on the beach, the leaf-greedy fire found nothing to feed on but clothes and photos. benjamin called writing *memory's theatre.* strut and fret. your dead slum the current trailing furs like film stars. there's a *performance* and a *haunting.* and you do not know the difference. *you* are traipsing the high-wire, dragging your heels in *fuck me* shoes along a silver line in the undisputed, depthless blue.

a brief history of the intoxicants industry in ireland and the americas

eddies of ice, commercial dirt. and i've no use for ravens, crows. a seagull is the white lieutenant of my grief. omnivorous fate i'm captain of. i gather my collapses now. ahead of me, you went. irreparable atlantic, air i dare not drink. the sea a lesser desert. gulls, my bedouin faction of the mad. the un-lamented moon upon a stick. an unrelenting labour. how the lung is tasked with blackening. and i've no use for crows. mangan, dragging his iambic backwards through a hedge, slapping the dust from his genius. behan, crying out in the quiet part of a coward play, like a man rising from an indifferent nightmare: *that's not what i wrote!* don't laugh. if you laugh i will never forgive you. i will smile, but i'll never forgive you. eddies of ice, this potbellied, sickly bliss. a bird as big as an unmade bed. seagull, squalid estuary of feathers, friend. white bird adrift in a damaged brain that cries to god. that stinks to heaven, that cries to god. even the protestants pity us. martin luther, drawing his horns back into his headache. the splinters asleep in the grain of a cross. i have counted them all. i have courted them all. i have risen wanting water, the lemon suck, a swifter shame. and ironed my smiles like school skirt pleats, folding my face through another day. no one must know. every ship in a bottle an ark, unpacking its animal magnets two-by-two. wolves come first, and last. resplendent wolves will inherit the world. they have eaten the meek. eddies of ice, my wriggling insomnia. a turretty empire, splendid, on fire. some fool, nailing his tongue to his nakedness, nailing his foot to his mouth, our lives to the rubbery suction of latex teats. you, before all. the cemeteries now, looking leafy and injured. minutely massacred, babies the graves will not suffer to hold. and i have no use for ravens. a million gulls are the roof of the world. for all to make a landfill of our language, actors arranging their teeth preparing to *do us pikey in different voices.* when you wore every slamming door, and a pio-neer pin, and a serious flag. here love, my most, mercenary rose. the lily that walks your lapel like a plank...

everything happens for a reason

the general mood is befouled defiance. the hazards are floating free of their fires. ugly girl with the high-top trainers has swallowed a song like a sword. it must come out again, somehow. oh you, fauxnician sailor, *all washed up.* your death is *so played out*, your long and tattered ceasing on a bloody beach in brighton. *liquidated.* yes, it was the sea inside that drowned you. walked away from us, from the jaundiced toil of cities, from a hurt so thick that you could stand your teaspoons up in it. weekends of clammy pique, bowing from the waist behind the yellow curtains, or sprawling in the local park, a patch of weak, white grass cordoned off like a violent crime. pit bulls, shit schools, cripple-lipped buskers slurring into their sinatra, driveways pubescent with weeds, cars on bricks. *yeah, imagine,* our cousin says sarcastically, *how could he stand to leave all this?* not leaving, then, but leaving me. streets, hampered and hunchbacked, eloquent with revenge. grenfell graffiti. drink distorting talk to politic in gutless pubs with drunken fuckboys chafing for a phrase in the hazy expanses of friday night. your worst thought was a desert and you walked out like a mystic and were gone. my cravings debase me: winter, the heirloom leaflessness of hedges, trees, dirty verges insisting their thistles. i have a *need* for pain, to stand facing the river, mulish and starveling. do you remember, the morning we lit the wood-burning stove on the barge? coffee, cigarettes, a cold day's slovenly currencies? do you remember the night we climbed the flyover? we thought we'd touch the sky, we thought we'd leave a footprint in its glittering physics. below us a swamp of lockjawed concrete. the empty motorway was waiting. predictably fatal, an estuary. fever ray's first album, a deep distance inclined to kestrels, the shape of a hare courting a hot pulse under an eye. you were starry, then, we made our own beauty. oh love, my only friend, i need you when no north is true. taking the train today, this latest vertical coffin accuses: *there are worse tragedies than yours.* i'm running, sunrise like inspiration porn, all pink-red-orange-captionable sky: *everything happens for a reason.* i have friends who say this. i am like london. cumaean, an unsuccessful suicide.

martyn / sibyl

the dead will take root anywhere, even here, when coughing up the old congested dread that wakes us on some roguish night or other when the saints have fled, and we will have no more of their composures or their pities. the dead will take root anywhere, even now, and with the smell of resin and the estuary, their smithereens are whisking on the methylated air. they say there is *no prayer* for our protection. equivocal deliverance, the only kind we're fitted for. agrarian provocateur! green fingered vivisector! god, who turns the corpsey furrows with a spade, and bids their bitter sap to rise in soil like instant coffee: fine and loose and dry. the dead will take root anywhere, surging again through the curdled mortar of pre-war houses, out into our dingy gardens, our small, obstreperous palates of stone. long night, lone, eavesdropped and seething, inclement with calamity, and i should know. i come out on the roof when the day is a blue lingering and sleep cannot contain me. i lie up there, awake for hours, and nurse the earache of their infrasound. on long nights, lone, of skirmishing cognition, i hear them, captive in the static like a warning of a storm. you hear them too, or heard, they wait beyond your vision *or* your reason. we were children. they believed a child could be beaten into sweetness. we were children, taught to walk with our hands in our sleeves, little girls gothic with patience, little boys walled up in their wariness. there are things we can't unsee, and you have lain awake, abandoned by god, sore with stomach ache and acid wrath, goose-bumped, grim, and bittering your innards in off-licence vinegar, insisting on the stinging cider piss that kisses you goodnight forever. there are things we can't unsee: the light in amber tangles struggling through tinted windows; the dead rising up from rural churches, shedding conjure dust and crumbs. they have no joy in them, or peace; they've heaven's corrective, affectionless love. whole congregations, dour-mouthed, and martyrs to the hardened artery, the pedants of disease, picking their scabs like delicate red and black brooches. you saw the woman too, standing without shoes or coat, opening an awkward scream like a wet umbrella, her hallway behind her, and framed for a moment like a hand held up in front of the sun. you saw the man whose face made mischief out of symmetry, wringing his wrists, flaunting a swollen jaw. there was that gaunt *aul' boy*, stumbling down the gallows path, his bindle of pious ailments high on his narrow back; a young girl hugging her threadbare errand, scallying and tousled, a hole in her cheek like a bad apple. you saw one other: the man who dragged an abject blanket like a baby brother, sucked the salt from flint to stave off hunger. he was *quite mad*. he called to us. we ran from him.

the dead will take root anywhere, they do not care for proverbs or precautions. i was a child, and i thought as a child, and i saw as a child: the whole world gold through penny-toffee cellophane. you and i, dissolving a sweet tooth in sugar. in summer i practised an endless piano; there were charioteers in plastic sandals, kicking up stones on the rathkeevin road. dogs in skinny gridlock, a piebald bitch like a broken plough was dragged along by her back legs. and you, running amok in jesuit plimsolls, ward of the state. you don't recall? the grownups spoke in whispers. i could not name the things i knew. you did not know the things you saw. the dead will take root anywhere, in endless heat, the living room, we shook the magic eight ball till the future fell out wild. the haywire logic of children: *what does it mean? we want to know.* and we ran to the sandy field, the rushy field, *the well below the valley.* always talking to ourselves, between ourselves, in pig latin, backslang, faltering cant. our pidgin words were ominous with inquest. names hovered like wrongful arrests. confession was forgetfulness, was giving up: *i want to forget,* you said. the scent of hedges, fuchsia, wet and red. the light and silence held my tongue. pregnable pause in the day's undoing. we mustn't speak, not yet. to emptiness: *i saw him there.*

they found his whistling head: large, and forced between two rocks. the head was singing like a kettle. the head was white and bloated, made from spit and paper. a nest, an egg, a lantern. they raised it up in a swaying light. a bird had broken open its eyes. *his* eyes. our dead are neither wise *nor* drowned. our dead will take root anywhere, as miscellaneous as weeds. you know this too; we're oracles of all the land is rife and sullen with. they worked you over for years, pilloried, imploring, from stairwells and from quarry bottoms, mutilated, stupouring. we *saw* him there. i won't pretend. you slip silently into their ranks, oh, regimental soldier. i am holy water, turning to dust. the aeons eat me. all alone in my in my flat ampulla. ours is a sour luck sucked like a lolly. this inheritance has no remedy.

of marat, etc.

to admire only the razor's solicitous dexterity, here in the half-light
cast by the loving of you. unswervable blessing, this *love*, this timid
word i rip along its scalloped edges. i'll observe a rare, a crouching
grace. old woman, rendered squat with prayer. cover all opinionated
instruments, their glow agrees a milky grief that trails its sleeves
through snow. i've no use for numbers now. the clock is diagnosing
midnight, loudly in the hall. this clouds the issue so, when here you
come! full of fledgling suddenness. the gulls arrive en masse. measure
of feather against your ghost. pillow, you puzzle sleep. dream, my
flights of utmost undesire. to admire your wrist, wrapped in its own
retreat. your hair, our tamest gold. and how your eye is winkled into
radiance, so wet and black and sly. i have leaned into the loving
of you. i learnt the names, committed your strict meat to memory.
luxurious carnivore, my least pronounceable animal. the grist,
and shuck, and *treyf* of you. your red specifics, squeamish, keen.
obedient porcelain teacup bone. the baffled curl. this circuit shorts.
i leaned into this learning, and the wrecked blade ran aground. little
ship. storm glut, your ribs are driftwood. first of all my dead, marred
and stretched, and here at your hungering limits, kissed. morning
makes its broke approach, dragging itself like a battered wife. beatific
pesticide, this light, this shrunk and fluttering holiness. to admire
the stricken and the ricochet, the warped hormonal loom of you,
the mouth downcast, the pen in a lax hand, pretender to the blank
page. where nothing is written. you've written nothing.

micheál / osiris

april conjures insult into symptom. i have often hated spring; this garden in its slow, perishable dominion. *mulo*, there are stale raisins on your grave; the black canal has set your bones like tar. you rave, and are peculiar to water. your eyes have met their lustering fate in moonlight; decay coerces pallid iridescence from the fine curve of your jaw. rib bone, hip bone, shoulder blade, vertebrae like delicate cufflinks. at night you climb the weary waves like stairs, you stare at me: *where is my golden crop, my flail; my grail, my golden girl?* your apparition augers *north*. your death has changed the sea.

i used to believe in *the one true god*, and with misguided gaze would offer my eyes to the stars. but you, my lover, are myth-mettled: osiris, bird masked for wran jag, adolescent demigod, all wingspan, antlers, and blasted sight. alright. therapist describing grief as shattered habit says that *nothing's gonna be the same.* he's wrong. every day will be the same day from now on. i will wander the earth in tedious hysteria, while you go grinning in a jackal-headed graceland. a crocodile cohort follows you, their cheekbones are sequinned, indelible tears. that's heaven: lig and swagger and righteous kingship. it makes as much sense as anything else. you will not return. i long to come to you, rehearse a wading fate in dirty water. i cannot drown for lack of stones to fill my pockets. there's only dust, sorrow's irresolute alchemy, putting pestle to pill, day after day. there is mourning, and all its etiquettes of affected modesty: the veil i dare not lift for fear my ravaged face would salt the earth and shock the little children into silence.

lover, i had searched for you, among the juiceless tubers, bulbs like little shrunken heads. i sought you out within the cushiony lungs of churches; ransacked all the wet black earth with clumsy, panting greed. my need was such i rubbed the brasses smooth. on my knees in nightclubs, graveyards, supermarkets. you were not there. i did not find you sleeping in the long, clerical shadow of a sundial, where once we sucked the soft grey thumbs of mushrooms to see god. i did not find you in the gold tooth of that prison *snitch*, or the nicotine pinch of his thin fingers as he witlessly plucked the lapel of my lagerfeld suit. i did not find you, orchidaceous in the botanical garden, inventing an eden by the sunken ravine where once we'd supped at doom's sharp savour. how i groped for your hand like a light switch in the dark! how we talked about *the end of the world as we know it.* i called to you, they said i'd cantered mad, clawing the spicy soil to pleats. maybe. there is a darkness we can neither stand against or swim. i searched for you. i searched and searched. death, an unmappable excess, distortion of geography. i tore my hair on building sites, listing in the shipwrecked kitchenettes of unplumbed houses. it was so cold. the wind got in between my ribs. i dug the loamy breadth of borders; pulled up those witchy fingers interlocked in secret charms to bring down chimneys: mandrake roots like sickly grasping infants. everything meant something then. tormentil and tansy, pennyroyal and yarrow. i searched for you, made inventory of ditches till the toiling eye was blind. i did not know it then, that you belonged to water. i know it now. oh, my love. rapunzel of the sleek electric tresses, let down your eels, your kelp, your skeins and your anemones. my gender-swapped ophelia, the worse for weeds, a crown of gothic corals for your head, and i could weep. here's violet pyrosoma for your pillow. the walls can talk. the river is unbroken, a taut skin stretched like truth. the black canal colluding in a sleep.

i remember everything now. *it's not an illness, it's an appetite with you*, he said. i hated him that day, the day i turned the tundra loose inside and sand poured through the windows. a desert isn't *empty*, the dead are of a nomad tribe. oh god, and is it shame that covers me, as certain seeds are covered? certain seeds are reliquaries, keepers of the tight green passing-sacred. if i should call out: *sink me deep*. if i should cry, besotted by the broken earth that tumbles me: *bury me now, and here, and last*. what of it? this passible delirium, a localised recoiling in the bone: *love*. they brought you home. i howled my fate. inconsolable horoscope. ides of march. i wanted to gather you in like swords, to dry you with my hair, to hold your blackened femur pointing inwards, grind against this sadness like a saw. it is a thin blue fire, grief. i will never fuck myself free of this, for all my leaden repertoire of magics: curses, cunnings, intuitions. if i could have one dazzling pin-prick minim of you, a single seed, a grain, to hold, behold. what then? i would take you inside myself. and i would give birth to birds, my love. i would give birth to birds.

intoxicana

i'm not who i am, and my uncharted face swims toward
him through the ether. he has no further use for me. enter
the brain's vestral spaces: here are a heap of mildewed
ghosts. the crease in an embroidered sleeve is black with
them, all black, quite wrinkled through. he says he wanted
courage, to uphold an inward breaking. we never knew:
every time we left we risked his ominous circuit closed.
some people cannot be alone. who are we to talk of *fault*
or *blame*? it is the quarter inch that drowns you. now she
studies me like her own reflection, with one hand holding
the cramped weight of an indestructible sin: *my tiny child*,
she says. death is a grim, protracted mothering. mother
knew best. the nurses are *thieves* and *vampires*, readers
over her shoulder. he called to me. at zero hour in *giddy*
heaven, called, but left me with the looping blare of grubby
feedback. canned static, or he spoke of suicide in thread-
needle whispers until his bluff was called, until the salt
air could not brace him. the body is an estuary, a sea
of several unmaskings. he *regretted nothing*. sinatra at his
most protestingly sodden. all his misled labours tending
here, the mirthless whim that had him dancing. dancing
like a headless statue. our dirt omissions. the ingenious
storm inside we feed. i'm not who i am. the way it wired
her jaw. the punctured sleep i barely lucked from. torn
waltz ending in a twisted ankle. and the mahjong click
of women's teeth. the failed decorums of our faith. you
don't know shit. and you can keep these reveries. i've
swallowed all i plan to.

cordelia at the home for the incurables / maestro

it has been said that i *suffer on purpose*; there is an art to that, and in an ugly soapstone vase the yellow rose aspires to texas not to sweetness. her fragrance is a craving you incline toward in vain. i swear i'm not *in love with pain*, but there is a splinter under my nail, and it is a piece of the *one true cross*. who has been bringing you flowers? and don't they know you cannot siphon life enough by suction through a cut? the rose is *trying* to grow, *trying* to stand on a snapped green tendon. oh, how sad. i crush her petals out of spite. we are alike. i also rush to water when i'm hurt. not to heal but borrow back forgetfulness, and every sink a sea in which my injuries are buoyed. if *love* becomes an unrecorded weight, there's joy in that, in going under, just the way some bodies melt like floes of ice. a rose that cannot feed can only float. and you, some luscious drug has caught you in its velvety fatigue. the rose has put its yellow on like armour. a paper boat with its paraffin seal.

how like yourself you are today, *not ill*, you said, but biologically beguiled. you've rolled around these pinkish-creamy walls for hours, like you are *the sound of the sea*. the hospice is mulling you over, concocts an unconvincing illness out of air. you *caught* this death, a salt wind under your sails. the water's meanest alibi. today your mind is cutlass-sharp and you could trim the white rind from a ten-foot wave. i didn't speak of *need* to you, or ask you if you'd ever loved a woman as the sea has loved: without fidelity or restraint. i did not ask you where you'd been or where you think you're going. yours is a sea of situations, not of places. *precision is the highest form of cruelty*. you speak of the land as a banishment. you have become prophetic. some depths cannot be reckoned: *some books are better drowned at birth*.

the doctor was stripping the flesh from a long, thin phrase with yellowy incisors. my love is the disaster by which i will measure all future emergencies.

a bad dream kneaded out of night, the mind's resplendent dark spectacular acute. fear has her flamboyancies, her oscillating logics. i cannot sleep tonight, but anger empties my head like a rush of sugar. i'm storm tossed in egyptian cotton, welter and tempest and cabriole. i'm in the garden, barefoot now, where sound curls into small convulsions, where noises make my shoulders shake. i am afraid, of everything. i am afraid for you, *of* you. sometimes i think: *you were the mask your sickness wore to gain my trust*. each man has an animal under his skin, keeps his disease in a private zoo. i caught it out in the corridor. you turned on me with a disfigured fury. hollywood gothic, reciprocal shock. an image of lon chaney, camp grotesque beneath the paris opera house. bygone gargoyle, muddy eyed. i bit into a scream. hysterical heroine. i gathered my panic into myself, withdrew like a threatened anemone: sudden shrinking suck intake of breath awake at last. *you tricked me!* an antisocial hour, rolling the moment end over end like a wet mattress. cowardice becomes a kind of violence, my friend. you would know this better than anyone.

to love, according to one's bond. to bleed out by a million meagre wounds. some will say *what bond? what wounds?* heretics are drowned as often as they're burned. people do not realise this. the sea is also an altar. these thoughts are formless. would you play lear? or prospero? oh no, your charm is soluble in water. i'd make a poor cordelia, am neither ariel nor miranda, fleet and guile-less girly-girl. caliban, my back like the bottom of a capsized boat. caliban, rising, barnacled, from the shallow end of the gene pool. shouldn't call you *father* but *master*. i have no father, detachable child, i become *stuck* on you. my service is a curse. test the sacrificial shape of my affection on the surf.

when i come in i bring with me the reek and tattle of a flammable world. the only news i have is bad: machetes are fretting, all bets are off. everything you do becomes deliberate now. *he's hurt himself again*, they said. but of course! you are a pirate, ripe for whatever mutinous escapade. i heard the nurses mut-tering: *a deep wound, yes, but clean. the way they'd say poor, but happy, or she's a dear girl, yes, but plain*. i'm embarrassed by the paper that i bring, the leering fate it folds between its sheets: faddy threat, conspicuous atrocity. you mither me for going *soft*. you needn't worry there old man, my days are made of enmity and vexed effort yet. i dance my gaunt attendance on a bad idea, daily. it isn't god i can't accept, it is his world. and even as we speak some woman is typing up a prissy-fingered list of all the ways i'm wrong. don't look at me like that. don't look at me to disentangle all your threads of lengthy error. don't look at me for anything. my own youth is disgusting to me. the doctor comes, he smiles like he's selling us something. when he talks he stands too close, i feel myself upholstered in his squeaky breath. he's checking his reflection in my tinted lenses. he swims the swimming eye in rose and gold.

the *cousins* came today, touting their preposterous fertility like lilies. they of-fered me a lift, but i'd rather walk, besieged by a green and crinkly heat, along stagnant canals in bovver boots. i can't make babies so i manufacture dras-ticness: buzzcut, eyeliner, a tattoo's grim calligraphies, and sweat, so much sweat. the cousins repeatedly checking their phones: predictive misery, a text that says a *nasty surprise* is the only kind that we've got coming, reading aloud from the local news: autistic boy is bitten by an adder in some communal garden, thieves on mopeds snatching up mobile conversations mid ill-fated plaint, a man stabbed in the face outside a high road offie. the day began with bad omens: the tissue i put through the wash with my best black jeans, the hairline crack in the bluegrass rarity my brother insists was *like that when i found it*. and now there's you, and how we drop words into you like children testing depth by throwing stones. the words fall down and down, we listen hard but you are bottomless now, somehow there's a hole through your eye to the centre of the earth. i've never seen you so emphatically haunted. in my dream last night you were peeling off your skin at the wrists like marigold gloves. your fingers poked up through flesh, long wands of coral awaiting rings.

there are some feelings not applicable to power-ballads, dear. when you said *if i wasn't stuck in this bed*, and i said *but you are, blanche, but you are in that bed!* and we had matching juice drinks, and you were sucking yours like a cut on the thumb, and i brought bananas which you described as *the acceptable face of fruit.* moments when your sickness is a kind of captivity, a cage you sing inside of like a huguenot canary. i astonish myself, i do not want it to end. it is less like *clipping your wings* than it is gluing your feet to the perch. little sparrow. little starling, insatiable among the scattered seeds. fear me. i hate myself today. i'm not here for you, i'm using you to fill the gaps inside of me. it is an ugly thought. send me away, i killed the others, i am not safe to love.

lucid but delusional, they tell me. i prefer *lateral minded*, days when memory becomes compressed air and paper snakes, when the dead slip from their gilded niches, grinny-gogging, unlamented, out for any irrational prank. you say *it is time to go*. but you don't mean *that*. you think we might decamp to the old marquee, throw our shadows into flying v's across the dance floor. hospital porters lumbering like landlords, and you can see ian on stage, along with every other tatterdemalion suicide bid the *biz* sicked up. musical loonies, they call to you like mermaids. sickness is an under the sea dance populated by savants and boggarts, prom kings with retro quiffs, by *our kinda people*. in a kelp-webbed haçienda tony wilson's waiting in a wedding dress that smells of youth dew, sentiment and oxidising metal. a brackish pint at the kim philby bar. a crust of salt around your mouth like mezcal shots. white worms, exhausted filaments. parasites that pick the seabed clean.

do you like my t-shirt? if i can keep you here just a little bit longer. if i can build a ladder out of logos, out of anthems. we talk about music, uniting bygone singers with their quaint old-timey suicides. who was the gun, and who shovelled pills? who took to a splinter of infected bone? sometimes i frighten myself with the narrowness of my desire. i'm still the same. i tell you *cars are* abandoned, *daughters are* deserted. it is true that i no longer expect better of people. we talk about what we *wanted*, and what we *intended*, how those two things are not the same. i *intended* to disappear, i *wanted* to be as thin as a crease in a white cotton shirt. and what *do* the beautiful people do when nakedness fails them? fucking: a stunt with buttons, the big reveal. i don't like men touching me. my clothes are flags. pull my pennants away and i'm a cage of contoured air. the forensics of undressing. there was a time i was raised from the bed like a peat bog body, a bronze age tool for cutting stone. an unkind archaeology, those hands. i find i can say all this to you, but only now. you don't like *any*body touching you. alone in the dark, developing your fetishes like photographs. in this we are the same. you said *the world does not belong to us.*

the world belongs to the *cousins*, those incorruptible pixelsmiths, perpetrators of precision. their iphones make adjustments for erasure. the young will learn to measure the world by what is missing, find beauty in a blank space the way a poem does. they'll filter us invisible. ugliness premeditates a ghost. *the camera was meant to preserve things too.* maybe this is better? who wants to be entombed in two-dimensions, with a shit haircut, in the past? the perfected image closes over us like water. a solid clump of turquoise, set in a silver band.

one to hunger, one to thirst. which is hardest? which is worst?

starvation was a winding path through a deep green forest. hunger is a compass and i followed him. i will not follow you.

some memories can jar the spine like whiplash: a mobile goes off, spraying us in the face with its melodious ultimatum: *don't you want me, baby?* no, quite frankly. the air conditioning on, old ladies led about by their dainty sickness, mincing and shrieking in turns, in slippers; a fat one, baby-janing it outside the showers, popping her pout like a pressure sore. it's hot. i require coffee so black it sucks the colour from our surroundings. you're like a legionnaire crawling for water, holding out your arms. when i think about being here i realise i am *accustomed*, not *resigned*. i cannot cry, my eyes are dry enough to chip the glass of lesser marbles. i've been here before. there's a sad familiarity, sits just the wrong side of contempt: chicory piss, the man in the next bed who is *so* fucking yellow, spread dead-centre like the hardest heel of cheese in a trap. the *sleepy heads* all welded to pillows, thin and flat as patties of meat. *empty heads*, unclassified conches through which the sea noodles again its contemptible eighties muzak. what? of course i'm angry! if i let myself love you, even for a moment i'd come apart like a dirty snowball. resentment is the only thing that's holding me together. you should see it outside: unswappable wives with rocks sewn into their bellies like wolves; junkies conjuring dithery mischief from flailing sleeves, and a narrow dog, whining at a bus stop, enticed to shy allegiance by the crumbs in my jeans pocket. *things are tough all over, cupcake*, someone has graffitied on the wall outside of spar. the man obliviously bloking into his headset, the girl in impractical sandals, her pink feet cooked and trussed like meat on the bone. conjunctive lull of afternoon, a haze around the houses. the busses stink, inside and out. a boy with pushpin spots, his face an angry mass of geo-tags. today you were wide-eyed and roundly abusive, ahab on adrenaline. captain of the *absolute*, or *infinite*. you have the profile of some roman general, embossed against the light. conquest is a currency. the dying understand this. immortalise your sneer in gold upon an obol. or do not ask to be remembered, close your eyes.

memory tends ticklish and i can't stop thinking: every roving focus, every slow dissolve. i'm sitting in saint saviour's, amateur catholic that i am. the evening lends itself to genuflections and to reveries. the saints all have the gridlocked middle-distance stares of drivers in rush hour traffic. they cannot help me. i close my eyes, reconstruct your oddly kiltered speech. *were* you trying to tell me something? death dangles juicelessly, posturing over its melancholies, pointing them east like warheads. this misery is too tactical to be quite sincere. a ministry of paranoias. this feeling will not be *avoided* or *embraced*. there is no progress, only repetition, the bossy logic of disease. and this afternoon i do believe that all the wet brains on the ward were weeping, choreographed like a fifties musical. the mind rises up on stilts like a festival funny man. the mind and its half-baked circus skill-set taking centre stage. i have nothing left to offer. i am bowling for bright ideas. every thought is a ninepin, meticulously skittled.

cry me a river. i couldn't come today. i couldn't make myself, i mean. i got pulled under a song and stayed in bed. i couldn't row myself to shore. now i'm getting coffee. girl i'm getting coffee from has an undelighted laugh. my last-ditch dirty jokes. her mouth is a blunt red pulse, wide and round with a new wound's promising succulence. i always liked to let my doom off its lead in a crowded room. i know that you do too. did. it's five o'clock, and the past tense is a *distinct* possibility. i want to run away forever, but i have no home to run from. i have £1.36 in change. there is no one to meet and nothing left to buy. there is no respite from the ethicless work of leaving, of being left. spineless ideation, and i said *every disappointment's like the first* – slurring fervour, squealing thrill – *like love.* and i said *i don't want to catastrophise...* but i do. i want the salty river's lick, a sleek limb in a silver gauntlet, carry me away, cry baby blue. i no longer expect better of people, have i said that already? i rage a lot. fathomless father, never one more worthy of the blame. i know you didn't ask for this, but i have clipped your silhouette and pasted it up among the stars on my ceiling between the bank robbers, squaddies, hunger artists. day by day your body looms, becomes ominous, prodigiously unappeased. i have been here before. and i understand mania's treacherous energy, how it is to be young, a stripling suitor to a living end you never bargained for, with all your brilliant schemes gone glittering up through a wet slit in your reason. once and future *enfant terrible* of the london underground, i know how it is to live by maladjusted tumult, black amusement, six a.m., when you cannot confront the former self you're shadow of. i wish that knowing knit things back together. as it is i'm slaking my slack mouth on prayer's brazen nectar. i think that pain might be your last great ostentation. playing the dane in a dunce's cap, a tricorne hat, half smiling. the moon is a tinfoil fascinator tonight, worn rakish in your honour. you are like the poor, you will always be with us. we resemble each other. you were a warrior, once, you'd grin and sink your teeth into any young and strutting error. my sorrow is a shore where things wash up. i wallow the received wisdom of the water, awaiting the change that is bound to come.

dead / sea / remix

in all my sad dreaming, where the sky is excessively sapphire; butterflies are fickle hinges, joining the world to the world. and i run my hand over the cow and feel her future meat singing through her flesh. as we climb the declining light like a ladder to the tor, to the car, to the fort above the bay, my memory has muddled this: the rain's tedious directionality, sleep's defeatist monotone, a man flourishing his misery like a royal flush. *in all my sad dreaming*, and the hillside hugs the heather to her superstitious bosom. people, their strenuous pity, my tears, at twelve, a long, silver brocade that runs from nose to wrist. my unhappiness is too robust, puny yet indelicate, and *no one can feel true sympathy for such an ugly child*. i think of it now, the sky above us like an olympic swimming pool, and i feel no pain. i could stay out here forever, the loose stars led astray in my telescope's lens, but i won't. a woman on a lichened bench coddles her pungent son, inhaling solvent gusts of him, showing him the broad and untranslated country: sudden drops, the sweet amoral prom-ise of the spring. she doesn't say *one day this will all be yours*. she says *you belong to the land*, because he does and so do we. *in all my sad dreaming*. i have let love lapse like an inherited religion. until the old woman spoke i had forgot i had loved you first. forgetting, in fact, is that of which my love consists. to be *fatherless*, to find no place for us among history's other spike banishments. in the back of my mind someone is always asking *how was this english broken, and who has broken it?* please, sir, it was like that when i got here. someone told me that you were *beautiful*. they used the word *stupendous*. they said your face necessitated websites. at a forum i went to men with the practised imper-sonal courtesy of airports wore t-shirts with your likeness on, your eyes are huge, your cheekbones embellished by infection. *like a model*. no, like some-thing you might whittle out of green wood. *in all my sad dreaming*. i come to the country precarious, tugging my ritual fringe. war doesn't horrify people half as much as the possibility that all wars will end forever. the president, bellowing his rapt decree into a camera. it's late now and wakefulness is horrifying. out here i feel we might mistake flight for strong drink and swal-low bluebirds, blackbirds, starlings, unmappable galaxy, augury, omen. our deaths await us like our unmade beds, fit to shame us. i loved you first. i cry for the little you belong to me, for having no name with which to orches-trate my own imperfect summons. if you'd come, here and now, out of the night, on the winding path above the headland, not beautiful, ambiguously derelict, and recognise me as your own. i'm far away now from the stupid ceremonious ecstasies of crowds. raise your arms to me, open my mouth pull the english out of me like silk scarves, an infected tooth, give me a word for when naming fails us, something to call you. *glory o, glory o.*

substance

a horned moon and the eye slides vacant / summer arranges her eyesores /
backaches / agues / you speak / with the sullen frailty of a child / you were
asleep / i was saying the rosary / a burlesque learnt by heart / gaunt syllables
of prayer / a novena / to saint rita / to saint martin / to saint agnes / how
you fill yourself / up with yourself / small god / the palm of your hand / flat
/ against the window's shivering grain / furtive faces of the holy family / sanc-
tified operatives / in a cold war / against logic / the body / and no one / the
tottering stink of the half-starved unwashed / bright distemper of an august
day / outside / a stumbled acre / coltsfoot and meadow grass / small green
spaces courting / london's small brown dogs / touched in the terrain / you
are / nettles and feathers / a hurt luck you flaunt and brood upon / by turns
/ and you were awake / and the mouth gapes fruitlessly / waits to discover its
function / then threshes its waking / with curses / old men rehearsing / their
sooty mortalities / sat in the garden / *pussy* me / my cigaretteless leanings
/ they came by their disasters honestly / omnivorously abject / in the blunt
convulsing light / of some know-nothing era / axes gambol toward / their re-
spective necks / fond / and then devoured / that's how it goes / *what a world* / i
should know / from the people who brought you weaponised malnourishment
/ who hang their wants like medals / who cringe in cells like white cresses /
wasting / yes / what a world / inversely proportionate / shadow of you / our
conversation / reeking / gnawed on / the bedrock loosens / and you gather
your teeth like amulets / disassembled / unassembled you / i cannot mourn
enough to meet this silence half way / return / to my time honoured agony /
to crisis and reprisals / bread so dear / life so cheap / and the drug / waiting
like some downright retribution / the fucking streets are awash with it.

Outro

Yes, there's something sentimental here, something over-the-top, silly even. In part it's a poetry collection read by a white-faced Baby Jane Hudson, or by Norma Desmond flinging herself at a Victorian chaise longue. There's violence in that, you know, a kind of weaponised hysteria, a mental self-indulgent flux that's utterly destructive. Or that's how it seems today. I change my mind about these poems often, except that it feels right, that they're here like this, now, together. Excess as aesthetic? Mode and commentary out of melodrama? Somebody called them Gurlesque once. Maybe that's true but not as we know it.

Other titles by Out-Spoken Press:

Epiphaneia
Richard Georges

Stage Invasion: Poetry & the Spoken Word Renaissance
Pete Bearder

The Neighbourhood
Hannah Lowe

Nascent
Vol 1: A BAME Anthology

Ways of Coping
Ollie O'Neill

The Games
Harry Josephine Giles

Songs My Enemy Taught Me
Joelle Taylor

To Sweeten Bitter
Raymond Antrobus

Dogtooth
Fran Lock

How You Might Know Me
Sabrina Mahfouz

Heterogeneous, New & Selected Poems
Anthony Anaxagorou

Titanic
Bridget Minamore

A Silence You Can Carry
Hibaq Osman

Email:
press@outspokenldn.com